A
Passage
to
Eternity

A
Passage
to
Eternity

Azmina Suleman

*A mystical account of a Near-Death Experience
and poetic journey into the Afterlife*

INKWATER PRESS
Portland, Oregon

Publisher: Inkwater Press
www.inkwaterpress.com

Paperback
ISBN-10 1-59299-801-1
ISBN-13 978-1-59229-801-2

Suleman, Azmina
A Passage to Eternity / Azmina Suleman.

    1.   Near-death experiences. 2.   Spiritual life — New Age movement. 3.   Suleman, Azmina.

Printed in the U.S.A.
All paper is acid free and meets ANSI standards for archival quality paper

12th Printing
Revised Edition

Dedication

I dedicate this book to
My Lord Ali,
my Mother Malek
who has been the guardian angel in my life,
my Father Sherali
who taught me the value of discipline,
my husband Amin
who has been my rock for the past twenty-seven years,
my sons Rahim and Shafin
who allowed me to pursue my dreams *most* of the time,
and to all those who prayed,
whether in Calgary, Orlando, Nairobi or Tripoli,
that I might live.

Acknowledgments

There have been many people in my life to whom I owe a deep debt of gratitude, without whose unmitigated love, support and encouragement this book would not have been written. First and foremost, I have to thank my mother Malek Mawani, for believing in me implicitly, as well as other members of my family for whole-heartedly supporting me in this endeavor. They include my sisters Shainaz Mawani, Rumina Mawani and Faiza Kaderali, my brother-in-law Ayiaz Kaderali, my brother Amin Mawani, my sister-in-law Asmat Mawani, and my nephews Rizwan and Aly. My deepest gratitude and fondest love also goes to my husband Amin and my sons Rahim and Shafin, for standing by me through thick and thin.

My heartfelt gratitude and love also goes to my sister-in-law Shaida Haji, as well as other members of my family including Nevin Mawani, Nizar Mawani, Amirali Haji, Gulzar Thawer, Zehrabai Virani, the late Shahbegum Nathoo, Husseinali Virani, Sadru Kassam and Akhbar Thawer.

My sincere thanks also go to members of the Shia Ismaili community in Orlando who provided round-the-clock support to my family, the medical and nursing staff at the Celebration Health Hospital in Orlando, and the Peter Lougheed Hospital in Calgary for their expert medical and compassionate care throughout my stay in hospital.

There is another group of people that deserves special mention — people who have always been there for me and supported me unconditionally in all my endeavors. They are my dear friends Nassim and Mohamed Jaffer, Zahir and Habiba Halari, Iqbal and Shehnaz Nurmohamed, Al-Karim and Shainoor Bandali, Azim and Shanaz Bhimji, Rustam and Shenaz Kassam, Parveen Maherali, Moyez and Rosemin Kotadia, Shamir Ladhani, Noor Maherali, Shairoze Damji, Irene Law, Arleen Frank, and the late Betty Dorn.

This book would not have been produced in its present format without the marketing expertise, design, editing assistance and encouragement from people such as Nusrat Hassam, Trish Romanchuk, Eli Schienberg and John King. My very special thanks go to them all.

Last but not least, I give thanks to God Almighty Allah, sustainer of all beings, for smoothing my passage through eternity and guiding me safely back from that Farther Shore.

Table of Contents

Foreword

Near-death experiences (NDE) are life-changing experiences that shake individuals to the very core of their being. Individuals frequently find themselves in a clinical crisis and it is often confusing or bewildering for them to undergo an experience that they do not fully understand, or know what to do with. These experiences go across age, gender, religion and vocational attributes that often make individuals question many different aspects of their lives. This is particularly true if they had a 'life review,' as well as encountered a profound religious or spiritual experience. This can be very unsettling to say the least. To best address the NDE and the physical and emotional health of the individual concerned, it becomes imperative that there be supportive provider staff and family knowledgeable in general on the subject of near-death experiences. This is particularly so for those who are not aware of what an NDE is, or have not considered the relevance of the spiritual dimension in their lives.

I have been personally educating healthcare providers and their families about their role in supporting near-death experiencers for thirty years, and one of the things that I have come to appreciate and realize is that the real teachers are the near-death experiencers themselves. Azmina is one of those incredible teachers. As a well-grounded and published journalist who shares her near-death experience in a special way and, in doing so, has bridged an important gap in describing some of the dimensional aspects that she encountered. She addresses such questions as what it means to have an NDE, and what happens on the other side. But, more importantly, she forces us to take a closer look at what it is that we should be learning and gathering from these experiences.

Azmina tells her story in stages and relates the meaning of each dimension as she unravels her story. She brings a very different perspective as a Muslim and someone from a multicultural background. Yet, she has managed to provide a balanced description of the experience without overstating her religious beliefs, and has only included those components that she felt were key to her experience and recovery. She has incorporated aspects of the support she received from her own community that were central to her experience, but also objectively communicates her experience for all to identify with.

Although there are other authors who have included the education component, such as PMH Atwater, many books and articles have simply relied on the heartfelt story. I believe the time has come to emphasize the *real* importance of what it all means — namely, what did the different aspects of the experience mean, and what are the lessons to be learned. More significantly, how are we going to educate more healthcare providers, teachers and clergymen to come forward with their support for their patients and charges — including children, who may also have undergone similar experiences?

Azmina's work comes across as one with great depth, feeling and honesty. She has managed to write an NDE book which is more than just her story that will satisfy the near-death experiencer, the healthcare provider, the researcher, as well as those just wanting to know more about the phenomena. It is a very well-written account, one that demonstrates how easily life can change in a matter of minutes and how important it is for all those individuals out there who have had an NDE to tell their story and be supported for doing it. It should also speak to the medical and nursing community caring for the critically ill. It should make them aware that there are, indeed, more things to consider than just the blood work and vital signs while caring for their patients. If patients survive a clinical crisis or death, it is important to understand *all* the dynamics that may have come into play during their crisis and not assume or believe that it was only the medical care that saved them.

Azmina pays special tribute in her book to the expert medical care and attention that she received during her two months in intensive care at the various medical institutions in Orlando and Calgary, but she also brings increased awareness of the spiritual dimension in our lives. She actively acknowledges the function of prayer, as well as the power of Divine will and intervention in her life that not only impacted her emotions in general, but her recovery in particular. Azmina Suleman has, to my mind, provided the reader with a unique and penetrating glimpse into the other side.

Dr. Diane K. Corcoran, Ph.D.,
Past President of IANDS,
International Association for Near-Death Studies

Introduction

Writing about my near-death experience has been one of the most challenging things that I have had to do in my life. Being an intensely private person, to have revealed my innermost thoughts and deepest convictions in this book has been to literally bare my soul to the world. As painful and as discomfiting as it has been for me, it is something that I felt absolutely driven to do in order to fulfill a higher mandate in my life.

The chance of being ridiculed and perhaps thought of as someone who had lost her marbles somewhere in the shuffle between life and death, is one that I have had to take for the sake of my truth. Writing this book, therefore, is not something that I have ventured into lightly. Nor have I tried to intentionally sensationalize what is, in fact, the "norm" in the higher realms of reality that I encountered.

In the five years that it took me to document my truth, I have come to recognize that you cannot intellectualize what, in essence, is ineffable and beyond the ken of normal human understanding. Trying to describe what I personally experienced in the spirit world is like bringing back a thimbleful of water from that vast and mighty Ocean of God. So, even though this book may provide a tiny glimpse into the higher dimensions of being to those who are open to it, it is by no means the entire experience — something that has to be *experienced* in order for it to be fully understood.

Coming face to face with your own death certainly has a way of changing your perspective on life. Often, it is only when something precious is taken away from you that you begin to appreciate what you have lost and realize its true worth. Therefore, coming back from the jaws of death has made me appreciate my life and the people in my life just that much more. It has added a renewed sense of purpose and meaning to my life, even as I continue to find greater meaning and a higher purpose in the everyday struggles that I face.

Undergoing a near-death experience, without a doubt, has forced me to re-evaluate my life and the fundamental beliefs in my life. After an initial period of psychological and spiritual readjustment, I seem to have undergone a major transformation in my psyche as well as my perception of life itself. More importantly, it has made me realize that death is not the end, but a means to a glorious end. Perhaps it is time for us to redefine the transitional phase in our lives that we call "death" — one that has such a ring of finality and fear associated with it. In my experience, riding into eternity and the so-called sunset of my life was nothing more than just a "continuance" or continuation of the evolutionary journey of my soul.

Strangely enough, going through the motions of dying has helped me make greater sense out of my life. It has, without a doubt, prompted me to live life more consciously and be more mindful of the consequences of my actions upon others, as well as myself, as I now have a greater appreciation of what really is at stake. So even though we cannot control how or when we die, at a conscious level at least, we can, however, control how we choose to live our lives. In fact, the type of *living* that we do directly affects our condition at "death." Ultimately, what matters is not how long we live, but how well and how honorably we have managed to live our lives.

Being ever-mindful of death is not a new or morbid fascination on my part, but something that every ancient religion or culture in the world has traditionally espoused. Cultivating a healthy awareness of death or the shortness and impermanence of our lives on Earth, actually makes us more aware of living. It helps draw certain invisible boundaries around our modes of behavior, and creates a greater awareness of the notion of personal accountability and rightful conduct towards others in society. Above all, it helps drive home to us the fact that we are, indeed, *spiritual* beings living a physical existence on earth. It also helps us realize that we are here strictly for a limited period of time, and for a definite purpose — namely, to "improve" upon that part of ourselves we cannot see, but which truly defines us and lives on at death.

Researching into the phenomenon of near-death experiences has made me realize that conviction is an important thing, something that is acquired through experience. It is the necessary element which converts abstract or theoretical knowledge into wisdom — not in the head, but in the region of the heart. Conviction, therefore, is knowledge or wisdom acquired through actual life experiences, and experience — for better or worse, seems to be that path to our understanding of life, as well as death.

Of course, it is one thing to experience the truth and quite another to live to tell that truth without appearing overly dramatic. I thus felt it crucial for me to verify the truth in my own mind first, before relating it to others and perhaps unwittingly leading them up that proverbial garden path. Therefore, without the necessary personal conviction, this book would definitely not have been written. Yet, with all the strange twists and turns that my life has taken to get me to this point, I have come to realize that writing this book was not a coincidence. It is something that has been produced very much by design, as I believe there is a definite method to the madness surrounding our lives.

While I have tried to weave the essential elements of my experience into the intrinsic fabric of this book, I am fully aware that I am just the human instrument or "weaver" who may appear skilled at spinning a good yarn. And then again, maybe not. To what extent anyone is willing or capable of buying into the full yardage of my truth is, of course, up to each individual. For my part, all I can say is that experiencing my own death has been one of the greatest blessings in my life. It has helped open my eyes to a rare and precious truth that, admittedly, can often seem stranger than fiction.

CHAPTER ONE

The Journey Home

The light shone out like a beacon. I felt like a winged moth relentlessly drawn towards the bright glow of a solitary lamp. Just for that split-second of a moment, it was as though time itself stood still. I could almost taste eternity ...

There was a hushed and almost eerie stillness to that cold winter's day. It was an uneasy calm, the kind that descends upon the Canadian prairies like a silent shadow in the night. Not a branch stirred on the leafless boughs of the poplar tree outside. Its slender limbs stood motionless, as though in silent prayer, as they reached heavenward into the steely gray of that early morning sky.

I breathed a sigh of relief as I gazed outside the partially frosted window of my bedroom. The howling winds from a few hours ago had died down to barely a whisper. As I took in the wintry scene below, I realized for the first time that I was genuinely glad to be escaping the cold harsh reality of a Canadian winter. I even found myself looking forward to spending two glorious, sun-filled weeks in Florida, in spite of the fact that I had initially set my heart on going to Hawaii. However, strong resistance from my two sons, then aged ten and twelve, together with a lack of viable flight connections to Hawaii had helped to considerably weaken my resolve.

Thus, it was with a keen sense of anticipation that I found myself *en route* to Disney World that particularly cold and frigid December morning in 1998. Thankfully, the severe weather and travel advisory from the night before had been lifted as gale-force conditions subsided to a flutter. High winds had managed to knock down power lines and uproot several trees along the way to the airport in the northeastern sector of the city. But we made it to the Calgary International Airport in good time, just under the mandatory two hours recommended for international flights out of the country.

The scene that greeted us at the airport bordered on chaos, over and above the usual hustle and bustle associated with a busy international airport. The foyer was jam-packed with people and the passenger lines backed all the way to the entrance, effectively blocking off several of the exit doors. We soon discovered that our flight to Orlando via Salt Lake City had been indefinitely grounded. The aircraft had sustained significant damage to one of its wings due to the high winds and turbulence it had encountered on its flight into Calgary.

Contending with flight delays and cancellations are an increasing reality of air travel today, but is especially the case during a busy Christmas season. Delta Airlines had, nevertheless, assured us that it was endeavoring to re-route all its passengers via other carriers pursuant to its affiliation agreements with those airlines. Although it appeared hopeful at first that we would make it into Orlando the same day, that hope quickly dwindled as precious minutes ticked away as we awaited our turns in the congested queues.

By the time we got to the check-in counter, we had managed to miss no less than three flights out of Calgary. The only remaining connection that could take us to Orlando was via California, which meant arriving into Orlando well past midnight. The other alternative, of course, was to cancel our trip altogether. Consequently, we had no choice but to make our way dejectedly to U.S. Customs & Immigration, resigned to a long wait both at the terminal and other points along the way.

The lengthy delays, the lack of choices and a drowning sense of inertia seemed to have a dulling and almost hypnotic effect on me. I seem to vaguely remember motioning my husband Amin on a sudden impulse, gesturing him that I would be back shortly as I disappeared into the crowds. Call it a gut feeling, super logic or just plain old female intuition, but something had compelled me to weave myself against the grain of the passenger traffic and wind up all the way back at the now-deserted Delta Airlines counter. The friendly-looking clerk who had directed us to an alternate airline earlier recognized me just as she was preparing to close down the counter. And it wasn't long before I found myself explaining our dilemma to her, of how we had missed several flights out of Calgary due to the long line-ups and time it took us to check-in our baggage.

The next thing I knew, I was being hurriedly re-issued four tickets on a Northwest carrier bound for Orlando. She had somehow managed to find exactly four seats on their Orlando flight via Minneapolis. The only problem was that all the passengers had already boarded the plane and it was preparing for take-off even as we spoke. She was, however, able to radio in the ground crew just in time for them to stall departure and personally escort us on board the plane.

After what felt like an eternity, I remember sinking thankfully into the soft padded comfort of my seat at the tail end of the plane. As I sat there in stunned silence, slowly going over the bizarre turn of events of a few hours ago in my mind, I could not quite believe that after what had seemed virtually hopeless, we were actually on our way to Florida.

After what turned out to be a smooth and uneventful take-off, I felt myself visibly relax. The turbulence at the back of the plane was a little more pronounced than what I was accustomed to, but that did not matter. What mattered was we were on our way to Orlando. Although unaware of it at the time, the hand of fate had already been dealt. I was being subtly guided towards my true destiny — one that would change my life forever.

Just as I settled into my seat and was preparing to close my weary eyes, blissfully unaware of what fate had in store for me, I felt a gentle tap on my shoulder. I was startled to see a young woman in her twenties seated to the left of me, next to the window. She was politely holding out an open pack of cherry-flavored chewing gum in a gesture of friendship. I couldn't help noticing that she was desperately clutching onto something in the palm of her other hand. I discovered it was a piece of 'worry-stone' that her friends had given to her for good luck. Although she seemed pleasant enough, she was also extremely restless and nervous. She soon confided that this was her first time on an airplane due to her great fear of flying.

As I watched my husband engaged in a verbal tussle with our two boys across the aisle from me, it became all too clear that the luxury of a few snatched moments of silence was not something I could look forward to on the flight. Even though I felt a little irritated by the incessant chatter of the young woman next to me, my heart soon went out to her. Before long, I found myself deliberately making small talk with her to help calm her fears and take her mind off the flight.

She continued to talk rapidly without pausing, and I soon found out that she came from the picturesque little town of Lake Louise, just north of Calgary, Alberta. It was a much frequented tourist spot and ski resort nestled in the heart of the Canadian Rockies, one that I had often visited myself. Before long, I found myself sharing information about myself, of how I had opted to become a writer after undergoing several surgeries to my knees. I also recall mentioning the successful launching of my first book in Calgary, just six weeks before.

The book entitled *'In the Name of Justice — Portrait of a Cowboy Judge,'* was a biography on Val Milvain, the former Chief Justice of the Trial Division of Alberta (1968-1979). Although she had never heard of the man, she nevertheless appreciated the fact that I had worked hard at producing the book. Spending Christmas in Florida, I confided, was a way of rewarding myself for the four long years of research that I had invested in the writing of the book. It was also a way for me to celebrate a meaningful achievement in my life with my family, something that I intended to fully savor and enjoy.

After a brief stopover and change of planes in Minneapolis, I was finally able to get a seat next to my husband and enjoy a few hours of uninterrupted peace and quiet. The remainder of the journey went without a hitch, and we actually made it into Orlando International Airport half an hour ahead of our original schedule.

Having visited Florida just two summers ago, we pretty much knew our way around the huge airport. By now we were sufficiently well-acquainted with the mandatory tipping policy at the airport and did not make the mistake of obliging every friendly porter that came along to offer his services. In fact, I was pleasantly surprised when a porter who had kindly directed us to our courtesy shuttle declined our generous tip. He said he was only too glad to have been of help as he graciously bid us an enjoyable stay in Florida.

I definitely noted a much kinder and gentler attitude in Orlando this time around as I found myself warming up to the people and general balminess of my environment. The air felt warm and mild, a welcome relief from the mind-numbing cold we had left behind only hours before. The gentle heat helped to thaw out and slowly infuse back to life my partially anesthetized senses. For some reason, I sensed a certain vibrancy and vitality in the air that I had not detected on my previous visit to Florida.

As I waited patiently outside the car depot for our rental car to arrive, I couldn't help noticing that the sky was beginning to turn a delicate rose, tinged in places with exquisite hints of gold. In the distance, I could make out the vague outline of what appeared to resemble an acacia tree — only it was not an acacia tree. It stood there in mute silence, dimly etched against the receding gold of a rapidly darkening sky that evoked fond memories of my childhood in Kenya.

By now the sun was beginning to set. As I knew only too well from my recollections of growing up in Kenya, darkness always descended swiftly and suddenly upon you in the tropics. By the time we left the rental depot, it was seven o'clock and the evening sky had already turned a deep indigo blue. The once familiar sound of crickets now punctuated the still tranquility of the night. It was a strangely comforting sound, one that had once been a nightly accompaniment to my sleep in the faraway days of my youth.

The shrill sound of crickets, the lush green foliage, the brightly-colored flowers, the temperate mildness, the exotic sunsets, and even the mild-mannered lizards that scampered about on the cement floor outside, all invoked a deep longing in my heart for Kenya — the place that I had called home for the first eighteen years of my life. In a strange sort of way, it almost felt like I had come home, a home away from the home that had once been Kenya.

* * *

The resort that we stayed at was owned by Disney and one that certainly lived up to its name. It was a cozy and well-appointed unit, tastefully decorated in soft coral and teal, with a separate entrance and private patio at the back. But its best feature, as I recall, was the fact that it was only minutes away from the shopping malls and major amenities, including Disney World. At least from this particular location there was less likelihood of our missing a crucial exit on the highway. I was swiftly reminded of our last trip to Orlando when we had ended up driving half the way to Tampa Bay, instead of Kissimmee — due, in large part, to my less than perfect vision and even poorer navigation skills in the dark!

After a night of fitful rest, our first morning in Orlando seemed filled with promise. Even the weather was more agreeable this time around, unlike the blistering heat of a summer ago. The morning sun felt pleasurably warm against my skin and the air outside was filled with the mellow sounds of nature. I could hear the soft rustle of leaves being interrupted here and there by the sharp trill of a bird in flight. And I couldn't help but marvel at the graceful agility of the colorful little butterflies that weaved noiselessly among the luxuriant foliage that surrounded our sun-drenched courtyard.

As I watched in wonder, it suddenly struck me that it is often during such seemingly mundane and commonplace moments as these that you experienced the true power of nature over your senses. And it is during these rare moments of pure unbridled reflection that you can almost feel yourself suspended in time and space and reach *beyond* yourself. Yes, it felt good to be alive — to be in close communion with Nature, and to feel vitally connected to something greater than yourself.

Our first day in Orlando was thus a slow and leisurely day that we spent browsing around for the usual T-shirts, trinkets and souvenirs. I remember picking up a couple of books that had caught my eye at a local book-store. One of them was a book by Betty J. Eadie that documented her highly personal account of a near-death experience that she had undergone nearly twenty-five years before. The other book — 'Kicking the Sugar Habit,' was something that I had hoped would help me make those more informed dietary choices in my life. In fact, I remember getting quite caught up in the book as I gently chided the boys about their junk food habits, even citing several pieces of nutritional trivia from the book. I must have managed to thoroughly bore everyone as the next thing I knew, I was being surreptitiously caught on videotape as a permanent remainder of our first day on vacation!

After what was essentially a relaxing day in Orlando, the next day started off on a decidedly sluggish note. I remember waking up feeling vaguely lethargic and a little under the weather. By the time I managed to drag myself out of bed, shower, and come down for breakfast, it was too late to visit *Universal Studios* where we had planned to spend the day. Having thus incurred the wrath and displeasure of all three men in my life, I was beginning to feel like a bit of an outcast and a spoilsport for ruining their holiday plans.

By late morning, however, as we drove into town for yet another day of sightseeing, my sense of guilt was beginning to give way to a feeling of distinct discomfort in the pit of my stomach. And by the time we reached that topsy-turvy building known as the *Ripley's Believe or Not Museum* next to the FAO SCHWARZ toy store, I was feeling positively ill. Thinking that it was just a bug I had picked up which would soon pass, I decided to ride it out and remain silent. Besides, I had to remind myself it was the first day of *Ramadan*, the Muslim holy month of fasting. Abstaining from food for the next few days could actually prove to be both physically and spiritually therapeutic in my case.

But after a few hours of suffering in silence, the pain and nausea began to escalate. I had no choice but to break my silence and ask Amin to drive me back to the resort. Once at the resort, the pain no longer resembled the mild stomach-ache that I had started out with, but began to feel more like the intense pain of childbirth. I recall throwing up something that resembled coffee grinds, which immediately alerted Amin to call the courtesy desk at the resort for help. And within minutes, I found myself being cautiously questioned and probed by the paramedics and rushed away in an ambulance to the nearest hospital.

Once at the Celebration Health Hospital in Orlando — the newly opened state-of-the-art health facility owned by Disney, I was put through a battery of tests. The cursory diagnosis of gallstones was ruled out when it became apparent that my gallbladder had been surgically removed a few years before. Since I was physically unable to keep down the thick barium mixture required for further diagnostic testing, Magnetic Resonance Imaging — or an MRI, remained my only option.

* * *

I have a vague recollection of being assisted into the MRI unit by a kind African-American nurse by the name of Carol. I recall her commiserating with me, telling me that I was very sick and that she would definitely be lighting a candle for me that night. Whatever happened next is a blur in my mind as I passed out in pain. The diagnosis of necrotizing pancreatitis and acute inflammation of the pancreas — a potentially grave and life-threatening disease, was nevertheless procured with the help of the MRI.

When I came to, I was surprised to find myself in Intensive Care, hooked up to several cleverly concealed monitors in the hospital room. Heavily sedated for the pain as I was, I was not quite fully aware of the seriousness of my condition and, as such, did not anticipate staying long in hospital. I recall making light of the situation, assuring Amin that there was no need for him to be stuck with me in hospital all day. I tried to convince him that I was fine, and that he should go ahead and visit the various theme parks in Disney World with the boys as planned. Of course, the mini-cruise that we were hoping to take to the Bahamas would have to wait.

By evening, however, the mood had changed. Gone was the optimism of a few hours ago. I felt dull and jaded, and incredibly weak. I seemed to waft in and out of consciousness and had difficulty breathing. The last thing I remember saying to Amin was whether he had managed to contact my mother in Calgary. I do not recall ever feeling this sick in my life and instinctively felt this fervent need for her prayers. I always set great store by my mother's prayers.

Whether or not I actually managed to reach for the buzzer and ring for help is not clear in my mind. But I remember sensing this sudden flurry of activity in my room in the middle of the night. My head was swimming. I could not breathe or move and found myself gasping desperately for air. I felt this urgent need to come up for air, but couldn't. I felt like I was drowning as I began to sink deeper and deeper into myself.

Even though I did not know it at the time, in addition to the significantly worsening pancreatitis, there was fluid in my lungs, my left lung had collapsed, my kidneys had failed, and I had gone into respiratory arrest. The picture could not have looked bleaker. I had stopped breathing and was literally fighting for my life. I could hear hurried words being exchanged around me, but the words did not seem to make any sense. All I could see was a sea of faces coming at me all at once, in slow motion, and as if through a wide-angled lens. Then everything seemed to suddenly go out of focus as I felt myself slowly recede into the background.

I could hear a dull droning sound in my head, like the sound of a washing machine nearing the end of its spin cycle. I felt totally mesmerized by the sound that was beginning to get increasingly louder. My head started to spin faster and faster as I found myself spinning rapidly out of control. I could feel an immense build-up of pressure on the top of my head, then a sudden rush of energy — like I was being sucked into a giant vacuum, and finally a quick soft release. I felt jubilant, like a newly-opened bottle of champagne that was gushing to overflowing. I could feel 'myself' begin to seep out of the physical confines of my body with fluid ease, just behind my forehead and the crown of my head. I lost consciousness as a great wave of darkness washed over me.

It must have been a while before I regained some sort of 'consciousness' and was surprised to find myself hovering over my bed next to the ceiling to the left. Although I felt no pain, I felt extremely light-headed, giddy and weak, like I just had the wind knocked out of me. I wondered what on earth I was doing suspended in mid-air near the ceiling. I remember glancing absently at the clock on the wall to the right, somewhere between the window and the bathroom door. It showed exactly three minutes past four in the morning.

It felt decidedly odd to be looking down upon myself in this dreamy and befuddled sort of way. It was like watching a three-dimensional movie of myself in which I could see myself lying on the bed, limp and lifeless like a piece of meat. I could see the doctors and medical team fervently trying to resuscitate me back to life. For some reason I felt a strange sense of detachment from the scene below. I just could not seem to identify with the seriousness of the situation, nor get emotionally drawn into the drama of it all. After all, the *real* 'me' floating near the ceiling, as light as a feather and as free as a bird, felt perfectly fine — even if a little wobbly.

As I hung around near the doorframe, I noticed that this lighter, gravity-defying version of myself even wore the same blue hospital gown with its grossly inadequate coverage that left a lot to be desired. I soon got bored of my surroundings and lost interest in the scene below. Like a bird that had just been released from captivity, I yearned to roam the wide open skies and explore my horizons. Incredibly, the mere thought or notion of it had the power to trigger a corresponding response within myself. And in the next instant, I found myself going through the hospital roof, like a knife through butter, and landing next to what looked like a church tower.

It was dark and hazy outside. I could just vaguely make out the dark silhouette of some trees in the distance against what appeared to be a moonless sky. As I stood there in my bare feet wondering what to do next, I became aware of a bright light in the sky directly ahead of me. It seemed to be getting increasingly closer and brighter by the second.

Everything around me looked surreal. It felt like I was in some kind of a fantastic dream, where I was flying around in my hospital gown. It never occurred to me — even for a moment — that this could be anything more than a strange or convoluted dream. It was, therefore, not something that I could get myself to take seriously, even as the full splendor of that inscrutable light beckoned to me with all its might.

* * *

The light shone out like a beacon. I felt like a winged moth relentlessly drawn towards the bright glow of a solitary lamp. Just for that split-second of a moment, it was as though time itself stood still. I could almost taste eternity. I felt the eager sense of adventure and anticipation of an intrepid traveler as

I surveyed the shining spectacle of light before me. And before I knew it, I found myself being swallowed effortlessly into the light that easily outshone a thousand noonday suns. But it did not feel like I was stepping into a vast emptiness of space. It felt like I was going some place definite.

Once inside what appeared to be a narrow tunnel, I was immediately enveloped in a soothing cocoon of love and warmth. It was a liquid kind of warmth that permeated every particle of my being. Also, it felt surprisingly less bright inside the tunnel than what had appeared to me from out-side. But it was a soft, self-generating kind of light, where the very space inside seemed luminous. Moreover, there did not seem to be any standing room in this confined but softly-lit space, and I soon found myself being molded into a semi-recumbent position along the length of this dim and narrow passageway of light reaching into the great cosmos. I recall noticing my bare feet, as I hugged my knees and rested my weary head on my lap. I felt exhausted, but safe.

Everything around me seemed bathed in a soft golden halo of light, and I found that I could actually see a little distance into the tunnel. At the same time, I was acutely aware of an intensely dark and visceral blackness encroaching upon me from the outside. As I willed myself to gaze directly into the shimmering light ahead, I realized for the first time that I was moving rapidly upwards on an incline at about forty-five degrees to the horizontal. I was travelling at what appeared to be the speed of light itself. It was like riding into eternity on the gossamer wings of light.

CHAPTER TWO

A Rude Awakening

My heart sank as I made the earth-shattering realization that this was not a dream. It slowly dawned on me that what I was experiencing was, indeed, the real thing, and that I was well and truly dead ...

I t was all over in a flash as I found myself straighten up and crest the top of a rapidly dispersing cloud. I could no longer see the world that I had left behind, as I emerged out of the tunnel and into the full-beamed brightness of the light outside. What surprised me was the fact that I was not casting any shadows and, for that matter, nor was anything else around me in what appeared to be a fantastic dream. But as I looked straight ahead, the sight that met my bedazzled eyes swiftly shattered any giddying mists of illusion still swirling around in my head.

It was *déjà vu* for me all over again, as I stared in sheer disbelief at the soft white sands glinting on the receding shoreline ahead. To my left was a narrow wall of imposing white cliffs, flanked by a broad expanse of bright green foliage against an intensely blue sky. And directly in front of me, in clear and breath-taking detail, was the exact replica of a scene I had envisaged in a dream just five months before. I had 'seen' myself drown in that dream even as I encountered the shining countenance of my Lord. I realized then, that I was 'dead' and no longer a part of the physical world.

I was also met by several deceased members of my family in the dream, including my mother-in-law whom I had never met or seen in real life except for in photographs. She had quietly informed me that they had been expecting me for some time as she motioned me towards a majestic white building in the distance. I could hear the distinctive strain of festive music coming from the building, where preparations appeared to be underway to celebrate my homecoming and arrival into the spirit world. As I approached the white building in my dream, I was surprised to discover that I could actually see right through the shining walls of the building on one side to the right.

Although I did not attach a lot of significance to my dreams at the time, I nevertheless realized that this particular dream from a few months ago had not been an ordinary dream. It was a precognitive dream, or what is often referred to as a 'dry run' dream, that had played itself out in my subconscious ahead of time — like a dress rehearsal, to help prepare me for some future event. It slowly registered upon my mind somewhere that dreaming of my own death was not a 'coincidence,' but a subtle message from my subconscious to help familiarize me with my impending 'death' — and the trauma associated with sudden death.

* * *

Ironically, reliving that prophetic dream and seeing those very same events unfold before my incredulous eyes served to immediately awaken me to the reality of my own death. My bubble had definitely burst. I felt totally deflated as I made the earth-shattering realization that this was *not* a dream. My heart sank as it slowly dawned on me that what I was experiencing was, indeed, the *real* thing, and that I was well and truly dead!

Gone now was the heady euphoria and sense of false security that had enveloped me so far. Up until now I had not, even for a moment, considered the possibility that I could be dead. I had just thought that it was all an incredible dream. Besides, I felt convinced that I was altogether too young to die as I still had so many unfulfilled dreams and ambitions yet to realize in my life. I now felt thoroughly miserable and cheated out of a life that I knew could have held much promise.

Although I had the distinct advantage of going through the motions of what it was like to die only months before in a dream, I could not help resent the fact that I had not been allowed to stay on earth a little while longer. They — or 'the powers that be' — could at least have waited till my boys were a little older before summoning me back, I had thought desolately to myself. Besides, the amount of time that I was asking for seemed miniscule, almost negligible, just a drop in the ocean compared to the timeless waters of eternity now stretched out endlessly before me.

I realized, however, I had no choice in the matter but to accept my fate and the finality of my death. As I glanced resignedly about me and at the scene immediately below me, I was surprised to see a large gathering of people — both male and female, assembling together purposefully in a clearing in the clouds to my right. The place was teaming with people and buzzing with a kind of excitement that reminded me of a typical first day back at school. The people seemed very relaxed, as though they had just come away from a long vacation or retreat, and were eager to take their place in this space in the clouds.

Unlike myself, the people in the clearing did not look like nervous 'new arrivals' trying to familiarize themselves with the vagaries of the spirit world. They looked like seasoned veterans who were once again preparing to venture forth into the physical world — one that I had recently left behind. Even though I could see them clearly, they seemed totally oblivious of my presence as they filed past three majestic-looking beings in flowing white robes and brown leather sandals. Whether or not they were 'angels,' I could not tell, but they had a distinct air of authority about them. They also had no wings to speak of, or at least none that I could see from my particular vantage point in the clouds.

For some reason, I immediately recognized this orderly

flow of people as being the 'mission line,' and even wondered what my *next* 'mission' would be — something that was probably several years into the future. At the same time, I got a definite sense of having executed my last mission. I had a vague feeling that it was somehow tied in with the writing of my last book on Chief Justice Milvain — one that I had launched less than two months before. Although it all seemed a little too 'coincidental,' and perhaps cutting it fine, I knew better than to argue with the greater wisdom of God's will and His overall plan for me.

The 'angels,' or men in white robes, appeared to be giving out final last minute reminders of some sort to the people gathered in front of them, prior to their embarkation onto earthly life. From what I could make out, they were trying to impress upon their subconscious mind the importance of recognizing those strange little 'coincidences' or mysterious signs from heaven that we so often tend to ignore or dismiss as 'chance.' In fact, I was surprised to discover that the relative success or failure of our so-called 'missions' in life often depended on how quickly we were able to recognize, and then *act* upon those signs, during our lifetime on Earth.

* * *

As I tried to grapple with what exactly my last 'mission' had entailed here in the middle of nowhere, I was quietly introduced to the world of direct telepathic communication. Mere words were not only superfluous but, indeed, seemed like an intrusion into my mind. Before long, the concept of what a mission is, and how it is tied in with one's personal growth among other things, began to form effortlessly in my mind.

A mission, I discovered, is not something that will necessarily set the world on fire. But it is essentially a set of *growth targets* that an individual needs to achieve during a given lifetime. In other words, *it targets the specific needs of a person in terms of growth in his or her character.* Therefore, in the grand scheme of things, it matters not what 'format' a mission takes. What matters, is the *qualities* that a person comes to acquire as a result of having engaged in a particular activity, or series of activities, during the course of his or her lifetime.

Then there is also that 'special' or dedicated mission, where the mission has a much wider and far-reaching influence that goes beyond the scope of the individual himself. Such a mission has the potential of dramatically improving the lot of the human condition as a whole. It helps raise human 'consciousness' in the world — as in the case of work carried out by the many messengers of God and geniuses of our time. They were all men, or women, on a mission who had, from time to time, been specifically sent to Earth to guide humanity along a certain path and revolutionize the thinking of their times.

But a mission in general, I discovered, is an exercise in self-development and personal growth, designed to help us improve upon our character. It is not a material or outward growth, but an *inner* growth in awareness which, although intangible, is the real reason for our existence on earth. Hence, it is this inner growth in our character and individual consciousness — namely, in the way we think, perceive and subsequently *act* that matters, and helps us get closer to achieving our so-called 'missions' in life.

Ultimately, how well we are able to execute our individual missions of growth and achieve our specific growth targets in life depends on how well we are able to 'act on cue.' In other words, those mysterious signs that we call 'coincidences,' hold the key to the relative success or failure of our missions on earth. In fact, I discovered that these chance occurrences that run haphazardly through our lives are not 'accidents' but *planned* events designed by a creative Intelligence to assist us in fulfilling our individual missions of growth.

Coincidences seem to somehow occur at a time when we are at a crossroads or turning point in our lives, and at a loss as to which way to turn. Often, it is during those times when we literally have our backs against the wall that we encounter these quiet little reminders from our subconscious. They may come to us by way of a hint in a dream, a gut feeling, or the sudden appearance of a particular object or critical piece of information into our lives that prompts us to make that 'right' decision.

Therefore, a coincidence essentially acts as a 'signpost' in our lives that subtly points us in a certain direction, which encourages us to choose one path over another. Generally speaking, recognizing the validity of such a sign, and then being courageous enough to act upon the synchronicity of events that may have presented themselves in our lives, is what helps us fast-track our growth.

However, it is important to realize that growth by its very nature is a step-by-step process. It is not something that can occur overnight, nor can it occur in a sterile and non-dynamic environment such as the spirit world — which is essentially one of constancy and non-change. I discovered that the so-called *'status quo'* of an individual soul is normally maintained in the spirit world after death, as it rests and recuperates from the storm and stress of earthly existence.

I further discovered that 'growth' can only take place on a physical third-dimensional plane such as the one that we call 'Earth' — one that not only resembles a veritable minefield, but seems deliberately strewn with challenges. Thus, in order for us to actively engage in our own growth process, it becomes necessary for us to once again become a part of a constantly-changing environment such as life on Earth provides.

One of the most important realizations that I made here was that 'change' — both in awareness of ourselves and our outer world, is what makes us grow. By the time we grow from an infant into a child, a teenager, an adult, a parent, and finally a grandparent, we have undergone multiple inner as well as outer changes in our lives. And it is this very aspect of change that forces us to *shift* in the way we think and perceive life and, more significantly, in the way we *act* and behave towards others. Thus, when we gradually begin to see life from a new and entirely different perspective, and start to act more responsibly towards others in society, we have in essence *grown.*

Therefore, until such time as our personal growth targets are met, we will continue to be faced with change in the form of new and increasingly diverse challenges in our lives. Consequently change remains the *only* constant in our lives, and is an inherent part of growing up. Life on earth, with its many struggles, hardships, pain, sorrow and temptations, then becomes the very platform upon which such growth can occur — one that is specifically equipped to provide the challenge of 'change' in our lives.

Our physical Earth thus becomes the testing ground, obstacle course, and 'school of hard-knocks' through which we can grow. It is specially designed to strengthen our spirit and character, and the very essence of who we are. In the same way as a physical muscle needs the challenge of increasingly higher levels of resistance in order for it to grow, so does our spirit. The moral fiber of our 'spiritual muscle,' too, requires the stimulation of greater challenge and change. In fact, the strength of this *inner* moral fiber in us grows directly in proportion to the amount of *outward* resistance we face in life, both in the form of struggle and change. Consequently, our hardest challenges often turn out to be the periods of greatest growth in our lives.

* * *

Life on earth, by definition, is one of struggle. It tests our mettle and the very stuff of our spirit — namely, that part of ourselves that we cannot see, but which truly defines the man. So, ultimately, what matters is not the material progress of man but whether or not his struggles in life have helped strengthen and bolster the moral fiber of his soul. Yet, ironically enough, it is often the material trappings of our physical world that blinds us to our true state — which is *spirit*. It distracts us from our main goal and purpose in life, namely, to grow in awareness of who we really are in the context of an 'unseen' God.

In that instant I grasped how life, with all its hardships, was truly a gift from God. I also saw how it was an opportunity we needed to welcome and openly embrace, as without the outer struggle that life provides, that inner spark in us could never be fanned into the full potential of the Flame that first gave it life.

In making this profound connection between life and our struggles on Earth, I realized that my own struggles in life, too, had not been entirely in vain. Up until now, I was still a little hazy on the finer points of my last 'mission' and what exactly it was that I had struggled with in life in order to grow. It soon became apparent as pertinent little details from the last seven years or so of my life began to flow rapidly into my mind. Unbeknown to me, they had also been the period of greatest growth in my life.

I began reliving the memory of how, even though I had never deliberately set out to be a writer, I had somehow managed to follow the right 'cues' and series of coincidences that had cropped up in my life. As a result, I had fallen into the writing process without being consciously aware of it. And I clearly recalled that time in 1991 when my Lord had appeared to me in an especially vivid dream, broadly indicating that I ought to pursue the path of writing. Even though I had not taken the dream too seriously, I did, nevertheless, enroll in a full-time course in journalism due, in large part, to a potential lay-off situation at work. As it turned out, I was never laid-off but did end up studying part-time and graduating with honors in the spring of 1994.

Although writing up until then had never been more than a hobby for me, the same year that I graduated I was forced to quit work as a legal assistant due to a bizarre injury to my knee that continues to persist to this day. And four years later, in 1998, I had not only managed to publish my first book, but also found myself checking into heaven within six to seven weeks of launching it!

Even though I was not aware of it at the time, my main avenue for growth at that point in my life had been through my role as a writer. Despite the odds in publishing my first book on Chief Justice Milvain, I had shown a determination and courage, as well as a hard work ethic that I might not have otherwise done. But, more importantly, it had helped me gain a solid insight into how a strong sense of ethics was not only the backbone and premise upon which our present-day system of judicial justice was based, but it was also the evolutionary force behind our *own* lives.

What seemed equally as important here was my intent or motive for writing the book. Fortunately for me, my work was perceived as a labor of love undertaken out of a genuine sense of affection and respect for Chief Justice Milvain — or the man I called 'Uncle Val.' Somehow, deep down, I had always felt that I was discharging a debt of gratitude that I felt I owed him but could not quite rationalize. At the same time, the very act of researching into his life had given me an extraordinary insight into some of the qualities that I might perhaps have lacked and needed to incorporate into the fabric of my own character. The end result was I had *grown* —

not so much for publishing a book in my name, but as a direct consequence of the impact that Uncle Val's particular attributes and character traits had had on my own character.

Thus, one of the most important realizations I made was that the key to our growth was understanding, and *experience* for better or worse seemed to be the direct path to that understanding. Moreover, there can be no single path to that understanding. Each of us, like actors on a stage, always have some measure of *choice* in selecting the various roles that we play or experiment with during the course of our lives on earth. But whatever the role, the end result is the same — namely, *growing through experience* and gaining a greater aware-ness of ourselves and the deeper purpose in our lives.

What was unequivocally driven home to me was the fact that we always had a 'choice.' What mattered, more than any-thing else, was how wisely and intelligently we exercised those choices or options in our lives. For example, in my case, had I not followed through with 'Plan A' as a writer, the next best but less efficacious role in the form of 'Plan B' would have automatically presented itself to me at that particular juncture in my life. I would then have ended up playing or 'acting out' an entirely different role, where my growth out-come would have been appreciably slower.

Even though there is always a 'Plan B' or even a 'Plan C' in place to accommodate the freewill choices of man, the first, namely the more difficult 'Plan A,' is usually the more effective and faster path to our growth. But whether or not everything goes according to 'plan' is, of course, entirely another matter. It is primarily dependent on the inherent skill and ability of the individual concerned.

Just as in the case of a video or electronic game, there are several different levels of play that we can engage in depending on our particular degree of proficiency. Yet, realistically, we tend to choose that level of play which we feel is closest to our particular level of skill and ability. Similarly, the role of a writer and researcher was something that I felt I was most capable of handling at the time, and was a choice that I had consciously made regardless of my growth outcome.

But more than even the writing, moving to England to study during my teens was one of the most pivotal periods of growth in my life. In later years, it was marriage and motherhood that had contributed to my growth as a person. In fact, parenthood, I discovered, is the oldest and most potent tool for growth as the level of challenge, sacrifice, selflessness and personal responsibility tends to increase very significantly in the life of an individual.

So while my writing had definitely contributed to my growth as a person, it had not been the only factor. It had, nevertheless, culminated in my reaching the highest potential for growth in my life up to that point. Consequently, I had not only managed to accomplish my 'mission' — or personal quota of growth targets required for my particular lifetime, but I was also legitimately in a position to return Home.

* * *

Receiving this direct mental feedback on what had gone on behind the scenes in my life helped me gain a clearer insight into my present predicament. This long and winding mono-logue in my mind definitely helped me connect the dots in my life. More than anything else, it helped awaken me to the truth about 'life' and that transitional phase we call 'death.'

I realized that mysterious allure of light on the hospital roof in Orlando had been my unmistakable clarion call of death, one that I had not recognized before but certainly did now. Yet, for some reason I got the distinct impression that I was being 'summoned' to the great beyond for some specific purpose — as opposed to being recalled for a respite and much needed rest from the toil of my earthly existence.

As all these thoughts started to crowd my mind, I began to get a genuine feel for some of the hidden dynamics at play in my life. And as I let my mind wander and momentarily disengage from the scene below, I found myself being veered off to the right in a powerful sweeping motion by an invisible force that I felt powerless to resist. And in the next instant, I found myself stationed in front of a huge translucent structure resembling a giant dome that seemed to be sculpted out of marble or some kind of white, luminous material. Even though I could see right through its walls, I could not hear what was being bandied around inside. More precisely, I did not yet seem to have the ability to tune into the higher telepathic thought waves of the occupants inside.

As I waited outside the dome, I felt totally cut off from the pulse of human existence that I had just left behind. At the same time, I did not feel that I rightly belonged to the glimmering world of shadowless reality in front of me. My sense of disconnection and non-belonging could have not been more complete. I felt completely and utterly isolated from all human as well as spiritual contact at this point. It was, without a doubt, the darkest night of my soul and the loneliest moment of my existence so far.

By now I knew I was dead to the world in a physical sense. Yet, what I was currently experiencing did not feel exactly like hell, nor did it feel quite like heaven. It felt like I was in a state of limbo, suspended somewhere between heaven and earth. As I agonized over my plight, I had a sudden flash of recognition. I realized that 'heaven' was not one homogenous mass of existence, but a multi-dimensional plane of layered existences. I further recognized that between each stratified level of reality existed a thin 'veil,' or void, that served to separate one reality from the next.

It now dawned on me that this immense vacuum in which I found myself was really a 'veil' or some kind of 'transitional zone' that exists between two dimensions. Technically, even the dimly-lit tunnel that I had emerged from was a 'veil' — one that separates our physical third-dimensional world of matter from the fourth-dimensional world of spirit. And it suddenly struck me that those who could not quite make it out of the tunnel into the light, but had instead lingered in its veiled darkness, were the ones who would actively experience the virtual misery and torment traditionally associated with 'hell.'

As 'fire and brimstone' and a wrathful God bent on vengeance have never formed a part of my system of beliefs, and since I tended to believe more in the inherent light and goodness of God, I was thankfully spared the tortures of hell. I was, nevertheless, acutely conscious of the fact that 'hell' was definitely a state of mind that did exist and was, in fact, very *real* for many. But it seemed to exist mostly for those individuals who did not believe in a higher power, nor felt themselves personally accountable to anyone for their actions in life. Consequently, they did as they pleased without regard to consequences as they let their passions and emotions to dominate and take control over their lives.

So although I knew I was not in hell *per se*, it was still a bit of an anti-climax to find myself trapped in this vast emptiness of space and no-man's land. Being in a veil was like being 'in transit' and I recognized that it, too, had a definite place in God's overall scheme of things. It helped to bridge that gap between dimensions and familiarize me with the inner workings of the next dimension.

* * *

One of the first things I noticed was that the primary consciousness of the *preceding* dimension still had the power to affect you in a veil, even though technically you were no longer a part of that dimension. In other words my 'ethereal double,' or this light and airy part of myself, floating about aimlessly in space still had the ability to feel the pull of earthly existence that I had freshly left behind. So even though I no longer possessed a solid 'physical' body to speak of, I could still feel the gnawing sensations of cold, thirst, hunger and fatigue.

In fact, I was now beginning to feel decidedly weak and irritable as the stress associated with being in a physical body continued to maintain its hold on me in this particular zone of trans-dimensional reality. I intuitively knew that until such time as I had crossed-over into the next dimension, it was something I would have to endure with dignity and grace.

This vacuum of nothingness that I found myself in was now beginning to visibly darken in response to my dismal mood. I felt chilled to the bone as I suddenly became over-come with an overwhelming sense of weariness. In looking back, I realized that the last half a dozen years or so of my life had been especially draining. All I wanted to do now was to close my eyes and drift off into that long and blissful sleep of forgetfulness. I knew that a round of well-earned celestial rest was something that all returning souls — like myself, could at least look forward to here.

For the time being though, I remember thinking that I would gladly settle for a warm blanket and something more solid than a cloud to sit on to rest my weary self. Seeing another human face wouldn't hurt either, I had thought wryly to myself. Amazingly, even before I had finished fanta-sizing about the creature comforts of 'home' on earth, I found myself being bundled up in a blanket and wheeled around in a wheelchair by someone that I recognized! It was my friend Parveen, the same friend whom I had half-jokingly bid to look me up in heaven if I ever happened to be on my deathbed, only *days* before leaving for Florida! Ironically, I had literally found myself at death's door within five days of uttering those fateful words.

As I tried to recollect my thoughts, it occurred to me that experiencing this fascinating paranormal stuff, and conjuring up images of people that I knew or desired to see was actually not that unusual. It was something that happened *automatically* on the fourth dimension. After all, I was halfway into the spirit world and in a place where one's innermost thoughts and desires tended to manifest instantly. Therefore, what I was witnessing was, in fact, the norm and really how life was projected on the higher realms of reality.

* * *

Whatever we experience on our third-dimensional Earth is channeled and recorded primarily through our physical senses — namely, through what we see, feel, touch, smell, hear and taste. However, on the higher dimensions, where we transcend the barriers of time and space, a whole new set of extra-sensory perceptions kick in and we now begin to experience reality more *directly*. For example, when we communicate, we communicate telepathically without the need for words. We are also able to 'see' into all segments of time and envision events from our past, present and future — without as much as opening our physical eyes.

In other words, what we see, feel, hear or think is experienced *immediately* on the higher planes of reality. Everything happens instantaneously as the concept of 'time' is virtually non-existent here. In fact, 'time,' I discovered, is something that has been specifically created for our environment on Earth by slowing down the rate of vibration of our thoughts. This 'slowing down' process allows us to, in effect, 'freeze frame' time — which, in turn, helps us organize and chronologically compartmentalize our thoughts into separate and distinct time slots.

Hence, it is this very separation and slowing down of events that gives us the illusion of 'time' — of experiencing a distinct past, present and future, when in reality 'time' on the higher realms is nothing but a *single* integrated sequence of events. That is, our past, our present and our future co-exists side-by-side in one continuous spool of eternity.

Due to this 'slowing down' of time on Earth, the inherent unity of the time and space continuum often seems stretched out, disconnected, and at odds with each other. As a result, there is always a 'time lag' to contend with on Earth *before* a desired thought can manifest itself into a tangible reality. Moreover, if the necessary time, effort and attention required to sustain a particular thought is not intense enough, the 'thought' can fizzle out and does not actually materialize. Therefore, along with the desired thought, there also needs to be sustained *effort* and attention to make that 'thought' a viable reality on our physical world of matter. This, however, is not the case in the higher realms of reality where 'time' ceases to exist and everything happens *instantly*.

'Thought' I discovered is the main ingredient and driving

force behind *all* manifested reality on Earth. But in the fourth-dimensional world — that is, the world immediately adjacent to our physical Earth, the concept of 'time' is non-existent. Therefore, as there is no 'time lag' to contend with on the higher dimensions as such, there is no real 'effort' required to crystallize a particular thought which manifests instantly. Consequently, everything appears 'effortless' in the spirit world and life seems relatively easy and uncomplicated compared to our struggling existence on Earth.

The fourth dimension is also the plane that most closely resembles life on Earth — but without the pain, the sorrow and the heartache that often accompanies it. And it is this very aspect of life without pain or struggle that gives rise to our conventional notions of *paradise* — namely, that land of milk and honey and life of indolent luxury. In reality though, it is just a *virtual* projection and gross materialization of what is quintessentially spirit.

Therefore, the fourth dimension as such is a plane of created 'thought-forms' — one that instantly molds itself to whatever 'thoughts' you entertain in your mind. It projects whatever it is that you wish or desire, and becomes an instant manifested reality for you and no one else, unless, of course, the other person also chooses to participate in your particular version of 'reality.' It remains 'real' for you as long as you can hold on to or maintain the thought that created your reality. But once you relinquish your attention and let go of that thought, your particular version of reality soon peters out and vanishes into thin air.

So, for better or worse, the fourth dimension is really a plane of illusion — much like a sorcerer's trick, or hypnotic suggestion that exists strictly in the eye or mind of the beholder. It is also the astral world of our imagination and dreams that requires no real effort on our part to conjure up. But it nevertheless exists, so long as there is some kind of mental or emotional attachment feeding the thought or image in our minds.

* * *

As I tried to gather my bearings, I figured that since I had clearly emerged out of the tunnel and into the light, I had to be in the next 'veil' up. I had to be in the 'veil' or void that separated the fourth dimension of instant thought-forms from perhaps an even higher dimension. Yet, from where I stood, it felt like I was caught in some kind of a time warp, or halfway house in heaven — where the view above seemed diametrically different from the view below.

As I looked below to the left of me, I could see several groups of self-absorbed individuals completely wrapped up in their fourth-dimensional world of created thought-forms. They seemed totally oblivious of my presence or the existence of anyone else outside their own reality. They appeared to be caught up in their own world and heaven of their making, stuck in their rigid beliefs of 'reality' and completely unaware of anything else existing outside their own little spheres of existence. From my perspective though, they were merely spinning their wheels as they chased after their illusions of fame, power and glory, and the utopian ideals of their self-made 'paradise.'

While I could clearly see the people amidst their self-created fantasies, they could not see me. But as I turned my gaze upwards, I once again found myself facing the imposing white marble structure that resembled a 'bubble dome.' I could only vaguely make out what was going on inside. A full session meeting in an informal courtroom setting appeared to be in progress. Although I could not quite fully grasp or comprehend what was going on inside, I felt a sudden sense of trepidation that I had not known before. I intuitively knew that what went on behind those closed but transparent doors would have the power to direct my destiny for the remainder of eternity.

Whether or not anyone was aware of my trembling presence outside, I could not tell. I felt totally shut off from the mainstream of human as well as spiritual existence. It was as though I had somehow managed to sneak into Heaven through the backdoor, and there was nobody Home to as much as acknowledge my existence. Yet, I knew I existed, not because I could plainly see and feel this ethereal version of myself, but because I was fully *conscious*. And as long as I thought, I knew I existed — and, as such, was living proof that human consciousness, indeed, survived bodily death.

CHAPTER THREE

Council of Elders

One of the Elders seated in front of me was holding out a piece of legal-looking paper and explaining to me – not through the medium of words but telepathically, that it was my 'life contract,' one that essentially granted me a new lease on life ...

*A*s I sat there waiting for the other shoe to drop, it ran through my mind somewhere that a meeting with 'the powers that be' — which certainly seemed imminent, normally took place at the entrance of the fifth dimension. I also recognized it as the forum in which my life would be closely examined, the outcome of which could effectively determine or seal my fate forever.

After what seemed like an eternity, I was finally summoned into the transparent dome. The set-up inside looked vaguely familiar as I recognized it to be the place where the Council of Elders ordinarily presided over the evaluation of one's life. Yet, I got the distinct impression that I was being summoned before this august committee not only for a review and assessment of my life, but for some other reason that I could not quite fathom. I was also acutely aware that being accorded an audience with the Council at this stage in the phase called 'death' was more a matter of privilege than of course.

In spite of finding myself in the company of others, I felt terribly alone — like a silent observer in a courtroom. Even though I did not take an active part in the discussions, I knew that I was the reason for their being there. Seated in front me on a raised dais were three serious-looking individuals who appeared to be in their seventies — two men and a woman. Each seemed to have a 'balanced' kind of composure that seemed neither male nor distinctively female, and each exuded a quiet air of wisdom and compassion that simply shone off their faces.

The woman, who was seated in the middle, appeared to be the chair and one guiding the proceedings. From what I could see, she was wearing a pale blue-gray gown that seemed to match the gray of her hair, which was loosely piled into a knot at the back of her neck. Of the three, I somehow felt an instant rapport and strong sense of kinship with her and felt emotionally comforted by her presence.

I realized that the bonds of affection that bind us to each other on Earth tend to carry over across time and space and into eternity itself. Just then, I caught a glimpse of a younger looking version of my Dad who had passed away twenty-seven years before. He appeared to be putting forward a proposal to the panel of Elders and seemed to be negotiating with them on my behalf. And as though to make a point, he had taken the liberty of calling upon someone that I knew and instantly recognized. It was none other than Val Milvain, the former Chief Justice of the Trial Division of Alberta whom I called 'Uncle Val,' whose biography I had recently published!

Seeing a hologram of my father in what appeared to be his early forties, attired in his familiar gray pants and open-necked white shirt, did not seem all that surprising. But the sight of a vibrant Uncle Val in his black judge's gown with its bright red trim caught me totally by surprise. He was the last person I would have expected to see here with my father as, after all, I did not have a real 'blood' connection with him like the one that I had shared with my father. Yet, for some reason, all my former insecurities about my present predicament began to melt away at the sight of these two individuals with whom I had shared great ties of affection and kinship. And for the first time since being awakened to the sobering truth of my death, I felt at peace with myself.

As I sat there dreamily oblivious of the proceedings before me, I was suddenly jerked out of my reverie. One of the Elders seated in front of me was holding out a piece of legal-looking paper and explaining — not through the medium of words but telepathically, that it was my 'life contract,' one that essentially granted me a new lease on life. It also meant that I had their seal of approval to proceed further.

But I found out that my 'new lease on life' came with strings attached, and was contingent upon certain conditions being met. The main stipulation was that if I chose to return to physical life at this point in time, it would require me to carry out a 'special' mission on their behalf — one that would also contribute to my growth as a person. The nature of the mission, however, was something that would be impressed directly upon my mind and revealed to me at the appropriate time.

This, to my mind, looked more like a plea bargaining session than a typical forum for reviewing my life. Also, for some inscrutable reason, it appeared that I was actually being afforded a *choice* in the matter of my life or death. In fact, as I recall, I was being given a few choices from which to make an appropriate selection. Amazingly, as I tried to make sense of all this, some of my life choices were projected before me in brief but tantalizing detail.

One option in particular stood out vividly in my mind. I remember seeing myself as a boy of about ten or so, flying a kite and living a life of privilege in what appeared to be a suburb of Montreal. But the option that held the greatest attraction, however, was the option to come back as *myself* — but with a slightly different focus. And I recognized that, for better or worse, coming back as the devil I knew seemed infinitely more appealing than the devil I didn't!

But coming back as myself seemed to have its own downside. It required a quick 'turnaround' and an immediate return to physical life. It also meant waiving that customary period of rest and reflection in the spirit world, and being faced with what could possibly be a long and arduous road to recovery.

By now I was so weary that I was past caring whether or not I ever returned to the physical world. I felt completely and utterly exhausted, and had more or less resigned myself to death. In fact, death seemed the more attractive alternative at the time as it represented a definite respite from those often harsh and incessant struggles in my life. All I wanted to do now was to go away some place quiet and rest my worn and battered self.

Even as I reflected upon how physically and emotionally draining life on earth could be, I found myself being guided into a quiet and secluded spot. I appeared to be in a closely wooded area brimming with the unspoiled beauty of bright green ferns and luxuriant undergrowth. And there before me, discreetly tucked away into the landscape, was a gently cascading waterfall that simply took my breath away. The water sparkled like crystal. Each drop of water seemed alive and vibrant and full of an indefinable energy that seemed to virtually leap out at me.

All my senses tingled in pure anticipation and wonder at having encountered such exquisite beauty. The next thing I knew, I found myself beneath the luminous spray of water that washed over me like the gently falling rain of an April shower. It felt like the soft caress of a dewdrop — almost like "fairy dust," that glittered and sparkled and seemed to melt upon contact. I could feel its vital energy being drawn and absorbed into every particle of my being as it cleansed the very essence of who I was.

It was pure exhilaration underneath this sparkling waterfall. I felt myself respond with every nerve and fiber of my being as I was cleansed of all my cares and worries, together with the extreme weariness that had wrapped around me like a heavy blanket. Up until now, I felt like I had been walking around in a trance like some kind of a zombie. Now I felt suddenly alive and inexplicably transformed with a sense of renewed vigor and vitality that I cannot describe. This was the closest that I had come to experiencing 'heaven' so far.

Quite apart from the purely energizing and invigorating effect of the 'glitter shower,' being in such serene surroundings was like a balm to my wounded soul. I have never known such tranquility in my life. It was as though I had just found my own personal bit of heaven and paradise. I felt totally rejuvenated and revitalized from the inside out. It was like taking a long and refreshing shower at the end of an especially weary day of travel. I now felt fully aglow, ready to take on even the ultimate challenge of once again venturing back to earthly life.

I do not know how long I remained in my newfound haven and sanctuary of pure bliss, but I could have stayed there forever. I discovered, however, that there is no such thing as 'forever' — at least, not in this particular part of heaven. I sensed that not until we make it back to the Source of all creation and become one with God's Light, can we experience the absolute oneness and unity of time that we call 'eternity' — or forever. Until then, I realized that there would always be some measure of time and space to contend with, even if only in a relative sense.

* * *

Although I recognized that the choice of whether or not to return back to my physical life on Earth was always mine and mine alone to make, I somehow got the impression that I was being emotionally manipulated into making that 'right' choice. And just like I had seen in a dream only months before, I found myself standing on the edge of a cloud and looking down over the top of a curved surface. As I directed my gaze past the layers of foamy-looking clouds, I could see what life was like for my family back on Earth as they tried to deal with the trauma and uncertainty of my impending death.

I could see my son Shafin, who was ten at the time, curled up in a fetal position and fast asleep on a chair at the Celebration Hospital in Orlando, Florida. He seemed firmly convinced in his mind that I was having a baby and was wondering what all the fuss was about. But the older of the two boys Rahim, then twelve, was more acutely aware of the true situation. I could see him desperately fight back the tears, trying to hide the anguish in his heart. I could also see the distraught figure of my husband standing over my comatose body, fervently praying that I not leave him and the boys just yet.

Emotions, I discovered, are felt much more deeply and intensely in the spirit world than on Earth. In a place where you can no longer feel physical pain, 'emotional' pain — the kind that literally sears your soul, more than makes up for that lack of physical suffering. Seeing my family in a state of such torment tugged heavily at my heartstrings and tore excruciatingly into my soul. My heart went out to them. I knew then exactly what it was that I had to do. Although I initially had mixed feelings about accepting the enormity of a mission that I did not comprehend, I did not anymore. I was also aware that whether or not I successfully came out of my coma would depend entirely on the decision that I made now. I knew then with absolute certainty in my heart that I wanted to once again be back with my family on Earth.

I no longer felt tired or lethargic but totally invigorated and mentally at the top of my game. I cannot recall ever feeling this alert and focused, or being able to think with such precision and clarity of purpose. As it became clear in my mind as to what it was that I wanted to do — of my own will and volition, I suddenly found myself in an enclosed space that reminded me of a planetarium.

The domed sides and ceiling resembled the continuous converging screen of an omniplex theater. And incredibly, projected there in front of me and all around me was the panoramic viewing of my entire life to date. Both the highs and the lows in my life were flashed before me at monumental speed. I seemed to be able to control the very speed with which I viewed my life merely by focusing and concentrating my thought. I could slow down any given moment in my life and literally step into it, even though it was something that had taken place many years before.

For some reason, I remember slowing down and zooming in into the time when I was a seven or eight-month-old baby. And I saw how as a baby I had managed to touch a certain individual, a close friend of my father's, who seemed to hold a special place in his heart for me. Every time he saw me, I could see him visibly 'light up' — something that I, too, had joyously responded to as a baby.

This demonstrated to me how, even as babies, we were capable of bringing immense joy, happiness and hope to others without being consciously aware of it. It also showed me how such love given out unconditionally has a way of kindling and warming even the most hardened heart. Pure love, I discovered, has a way of sparking off a connection at the deepest and innermost part of ourselves — one that is essentially spirit, or *light*.

Rather than dwelling on the events themselves, what seemed important here was the net outcome of events — namely, how my particular actions in life had affected *others*. As a result, I was able to gain valuable insight into how other people perceived me, something that I had not always been aware of before. It was like viewing my entire life from several angles all at once, and from a wider than usual perspective. What surprised me was the fact that what I had considered relatively trivial, or insignificant, often had a more profound and far-reaching effect on my life than something that I had thought was really important. In fact, I realized that I had learned more valuable life lessons from my failures than the apparent 'successes' in my life.

* * *

My life review seemed over in a flash. Not a detail was missed as I saw the truth behind every event in my life in a way that I would never have thought was possible. Interestingly enough, it was not a matter of anyone else judging my life, but *me* examining my own life and then judging myself accordingly. I discovered that not only was I the sole judge and arbiter of my own life, but also my harshest critic. And wherever my conscience pricked the most, that was the area in my life that had the greatest scope for improvement.

Ultimately, I saw that how much light I was able to shed on the errors and omissions in my life really boiled down to how much of that precious commodity called 'conscience' I possessed. Moreover, I found out that the intuitive wisdom of that 'small voice within' — one that helps us discern right from wrong, does not necessarily emanate from the head but flows from the *heart*. It is a type of 'emotional intelligence' that requires the head to connect with the heart in order to activate its flow. Hence, I discovered that it is not only the theoretical knowledge floating around in our head that counts, but the wisdom that comes from deep within our heart and the very seat of our soul.

In the end, what really matters is the 'inner' condition of our heart. What counts is how well we are able to *think* with our heart and hear the softly-spoken wisdom of our soul. More than anything else, it is the clarity of this 'inner voice' in us that remains the true yardstick for determining how well we measure up to others — and, indeed, ourselves.

The main purpose of undergoing a life review, I saw, was to help me 'examine myself' in the light of my own conscience, in the light of complete truth and honesty. It was a way for me to find out some hardcore truths about myself — without being able to hide behind the façade of my self-delusions, deceptions or lies, and see what it was that I had done that was of any *real* consequence in my life. Consequently, being put under the microscope of scrutiny of my own conscience — or 'higher' self, helped me to clearly see and feel the error of my ways. It helped me to seriously reflect upon my actions in life, prompting me to amend my ways and resolve to do better in the future.

Growth or evolution by nature is a step-by-step process. It is much easier to remedy a situation by implementing minor changes along the way, and getting back on track earlier on in the game than later. Hence, I recognized that the true value of undergoing a life review is the awareness and clarity it brings by shining that light of scrutiny upon our faults and deviations that we are so often blinded to in life. Awareness, therefore, becomes the critical first step towards self-improvement and reformation — which, really, is the whole point of evolution and life itself.

Without taking the time to stop, reflect and occasionally check our bearings, we would forever be meandering in the process that we call 'life.' A life review, therefore, acts as a quick reality check that tells us at a glance exactly how far along we are on that slippery slope of evolution, and how much further we have yet to go. It basically informs us as to whether or not we are on track, off course, or generally headed in the right direction.

A critique or self-assessment of our lives, therefore, helps us focus and redirect our energy towards our true purpose in life. It allows us to see the forest for the trees and gain a clearer perspective, both on ourselves as well as our ultimate destination. Above all, it helps steer us Home in a pristine enough state worthy of our Maker. Put another way, it allows us to see the 'big picture' and set our sights firmly on the prize — namely, that of becoming one with God.

* * *

Even though I was alone throughout the life review process, I was somehow always conscious of the comforting presence of my Lord by my side. He did not intervene, nor did He intrude upon the proceedings. Rather than dictate or manipulate, His presence helped me focus. His sole purpose was to guide me through the transition between my physical life and the 'true' life, by showing me the way and pointing me towards that 'right' path.

It was made abundantly clear to me from the start that the necessary effort and initiative required to stay on track could only come from myself, and no one else. And so whether or not I chose to follow my Master's direction, was clearly a matter of my own freewill choice as there could never be any force or coercion in matters of true spiritual salvation. I realized that, ultimately, the urge or compulsion to do the 'right' thing had to come from within myself. In the end, the only person that could stop me from sticking to 'the straight and narrow' and straying off course was none other than *myself* — namely, my willful and obdurate self!

Even as I gathered rapid insight into the truth about myself and my passage through eternity, it was gently brought to my attention that I had 'gained.' Riding as I was on my roller coaster of emotions, alternating between the great heights of joy and depths of despair, this was music to my ears! I was immensely happy — nay, ecstatic. I had actually managed to gain ground on the forward thrust of evolution.

This was, indeed, my self-defining moment — something that lies at the heart of evolution itself. What it basically amounted to, in real terms, was that I had evolved as a direct result of the very struggles and challenges that I had faced in life. More importantly, it confirmed to me that my life to date had not been in vain. It appeared that I had effectively achieved my "mission" — or quota of personal growth targets allocated towards my life thus far. Consequently, I was now at liberty to map out and plot the *future* course of my life, along with a fresh list of growth objectives necessary for the further development of my soul and growth as an individual.

As though on cue and to graphically drive the point home to me, I found myself standing at the helm of a ship poring over some maps and deliberately trying to navigate my craft along what looked like the uncharted waters of my life. In that instant, I instinctively knew that if I steered my craft along a certain path — one that was clearly being pointed out to me, I would most definitely hit 'land.' As I made this startling discovery, I felt my gaze being compellingly directed towards the far horizon and illuminated Shores of my final destination.

From where I stood, it looked like I had about half a day's journey ahead of me — roughly equivalent to half a lifetime on earth. It suddenly hit me with an overwhelming sense of certainty that my new 'mission' had the potential of helping me reach that farther Shore. Indeed, if I played my cards right, I had the very real ability to break through into the final dimensions of being. I realized that I had the power to once and for all free myself from the shackles of earthly human bondage — or that vicious cycle of birth and rebirth known as reincarnation.

Although I did not know at the time what exactly my new 'mission' would entail, I now seemed to have a better sense of destiny as well as an added impetus to return. From what I could make out, I had the potential of making this my final lap on the wheel of life. Thus, summoning the courage to return to Earth seemed much more appealing now. I could, in essence, kill two birds with one stone — I could be with my family once again, and at the same time have the opportunity to improve upon myself enough to make it to that elusive farther Shore.

I recognized, however, that to act upon this opportunity required a quick 'turnaround' from the phase called 'death' — one that I was actively experiencing. It also meant temporarily waiving my God-given right to that welcome period of celestial rest and returning to Earth *immediately* — as opposed to some indeterminate time in the future. Either way, I was acutely aware of the fact that the decision to stay in the spirit world, or return to physical life, always remained mine and mine alone to make.

* * *

I feel singularly blessed to have had the opportunity to examine my life in the clearest light possible. As a result, I seem to possess a longer range view of both my physical as well as spiritual life. But more than anything else, I can remember feeling this overwhelming sense of gratitude and joy for having been given a *choice* in the matter of my life and death itself. And as strange as it may sound, I can even recall that precise moment in my life when I was first made aware of the possibility of such a choice looming up in my life.

In that instant, I found myself flash back to that fateful day in 1991 when I was first afforded a flitting glimpse into my future. I recall confiding in Arleen, a dear friend at the office with whom I shared office space and such confidences, about a haunting premonition that I had that I just could not seem to shake off. I had tearfully revealed to her that I had this nagging feeling that I only had a handful more years to live, and had agonized over leaving behind my husband and two children, then just six and four.

Although I had tried to subsequently convince myself that it was just the product of an overactive imagination, deep down in my heart I knew then, as I know now, where exactly it was that I was headed. I was headed Home towards the blazing glory of that Farther Shore.

CHAPTER FOUR

God's Magic Kingdom

Immediately ahead was a broad beam of light that was beginning to descend slowly downwards and fuse with the upper stratosphere of space above me. Then from within that solitary ray of brilliance, I saw several of God's Messengers manifest themselves before me in all their shining glory ...

*A*s I gazed into the horizon, I could see a distinctive blue haze gathering in the distance that was coming increasingly closer. Then suddenly, without warning, something quite extraordinary started to unfold around me. All my senses seemed to come alive as I witnessed several "flashbulbs" of light explode dazzlingly over my face. And there, before me, stood several indistinguishable figures enshrouded in an ethereal blue light which were slowly beginning to materialize out of the mist.

Whatever I sensed, felt or thought at this point seemed to bounce directly off the chart of my consciousness and trail-off into tiny explosions of light. Everything seemed to happen all at once, as events started to quicken and blend into each other. At least that is the way it appeared to me on this plane of rapid vibrations where time itself seemed non-existent. Therefore, the account that follows is a deliberately slowed down sequence of events that occurred *simultaneously* — in a single moment of expanded time.

* * *

I could not quite believe my eyes as I began to slowly recognize some of the individuals before me. At the head of the group stood the gaunt and hunched figure of the social activist and freedom fighter, Mahatma Gandhi. Standing next to him, dressed in a plain white sari with her hands clasped serenely in prayer, was the figure of a white Caucasian woman. It was not until several months later that I was able to uncover her true identity — an English woman by the name of Madeleine Slade, also known as *Mira Behn*, who had been a devout supporter of Gandhi's.

Immediately below them was the charismatic figure of Martin Luther King, Jr., the black pacifist and civil rights leader from the 1960's. He was followed by the striking and impressive figures of the legendary Greek god, Zeus, and that mythical Egyptian sun god, Amon-Ra — both of whom I immediately recognized from my history books in elementary school.

On the outer edge of the group to the left stood a tall and lanky Native American with deeply chiseled features, dark hair, and a single feather on his head. Even though I was not able to identify him at the time, upon a review of several native Indian chiefs a few years later, I recognized him to be Chief Crowfoot of the Blackfoot tribe in southern Alberta. Like Gandhi, I learned that Crowfoot too had believed in non-violence and, coincidentally, was also known as the 'Father of his people.'

To the extreme right of the group sat the lone and cross-legged figure of an East Indian swami, or holy man, who reminded me of a Buddhist priest. He had a piece of white loincloth draped around his waist, a string of black beads around his neck, and a distinctive marking on his forehead. I have not to this day been able to identify this individual.

As I watched these figures of historical renown with great interest, understanding began to flood my mind. I realized that the individual flashes of light that had preceded their physical manifestation represented their *inner light*, or spark of the divine in each of the individuals now before me. In my present state of consciousness, it seemed that I required the familiarity of color and form in order for me to recognize them more fully. As I could not yet distinguish them solely by the brilliance of their inner light, they had to considerably 'power down' their vibrations in order for me to identify them as human beings who once walked the Earth.

Even though I could not recognize all the figures in the group at the time, what baffled me was the fact that an

Egyptian sun god, together with a *two-headed* Greek god, had never formed a part of my system of beliefs in life. I had always considered that sort of thing the stuff of myth and legend — something that belonged in the realm of fiction and pure hypothetical conjecture.

Seeing a two-headed Greek god with a perfectly formed *female* head seemed almost too ludicrous for me to consider. This is where I knew I had to draw the line. None of this could be *real* I told myself — just a serious case of my mind playing tricks on me! How else could I have conjured up a two-headed mythical god that I did not believe in, or a sun god who was not a part of my repertoire of beliefs. In fact, it definitely crossed my mind that I was perhaps barking up the wrong tree in heaven, as the 'reality' out there was certainly not what I had envisioned it to be.

No sooner had I cast doubt upon the very nature of my 'reality' and allowed it to seep unbidden into the bedrock of my consciousness, I started to feel the core and foundation of what I considered to be my safe notions of reality begin to crumble and shatter into a million pieces. In the same instant, the words 'Think *again*' began to reverberate resoundingly in my mind, beckoning me to look *beyond* the narrow confines of my mind and splintered pieces of consciousness.

Strangely enough, the fact that I had 'seen' a couple of mythical figures that did not fit into my picture of 'reality' made me begrudgingly acknowledge the fact that there *could* perhaps be other realities out there that I was simply not aware of. It also crossed my mind that I was now no longer able to project my *own* somewhat logically ordered thoughts onto this particular zone of reality. It appeared that I had

somehow managed to transcend the fourth-dimensional landscape of created 'thought-forms' and my so-called "paradise."

I had always known at some level of consciousness that
the notion of "paradise" was an illusion. It was nothing more
than a 'projection' of my *own* thoughts and desires — just a
temporal and fickle thing capable of vanishing into thin air
like some magician's trick. But I also instinctively knew that
behind the "smoke and mirrors" of the fourth dimension lay
a definite spark of reality — something that was not only
infinitely more real and enduring, but transcended our very
notions of thought as well as form.

* * *

It suddenly occurred to me that I was now *behind* the "smoke
and mirrors" of the fourth dimension as I found myself
moving purposefully towards the inner core of the next
dimension — a dimension that exists independent of desire
and thought. I was surprised to discover that I had managed
to cross-over into the fifth dimension with such relative ease.
I sensed that I was now in an altogether different branch of
heaven — one that had, until now, been clearly outside my
range of conscious experience.

As I opened myself to the possibility of encountering new
and greater realms of existence, something extraordinary
started to take place around me. Not only was the truth
emblazoned directly upon my soul, but I began to *experience*
that truth with the full force of a lightning strike.

I found myself being totally mesmerized and captivated by an array of golden white lights streaking into the heavens. As the lights drew closer, I saw what looked like huge "fireballs" of light explode all over me and completely envelop me with their brilliance. It was like witnessing a magnificent display of fireworks, only to realize that I was also the core and center-piece of that dazzling display of light. Curiously, this meteoric spectacle of lights was not only coming from all around me, but also from *within* me.

As I gazed over the edge of the broad canvas of clouds, I could see scattered pinpricks of light flickering steadily in the distance. Some were dancing around like fireflies, while others were more isolated and spread out like tiny little glow worms blinking in the half-light. It was like looking *down* on a star-studded sky instead of up, where each individual star seemed to be emitting back a definite degree of light and brilliance.

It suddenly occurred to me that this breathtaking mosaic of lights collectively represented the individual sparks of light that dwell within each and every living thing on earth. Those who were aware of this light in their hearts — even if only in a vague sort of way, and were earnestly attempting to connect with God or a Higher Intelligence through thought or prayer, seemed to somehow glow brighter.

Then in a flash of pure understanding, I began to grasp the stupendous power of prayer. I saw how prayer was really a formal act of remembrance of God, or a Higher Intelligence, by whatever name we chose to call Him. It was the vital means through which an individual soul communicated with its Creator. In a strange sort of way, it reminded me of

Stephen Spielberg's 'E.T.' — that extra-terrestrial who had an inborn need to call Home and connect with his Mothership. And it struck me, it mattered not what we called our Creator — *just so long as we called,* as there is, indeed, only ONE God who answers all our prayers.

God makes no distinction between Christian, Muslim, Jewish, Hindu or any other kind of prayer. He hears them equally. Any prayer that is said in earnest, in humility, and with a loving heart, has the same power and effect as any other prayer — whatever its language, or mode of delivery. Just as fresh water is essential for our physical survival on earth — whatever its source, prayer, too, is essential for the spiritual sustenance of our souls, regardless of the language or what form the prayer may take.

But the purest form of prayer, I discovered, is one that is not tainted with thoughts of 'self' but submitted out of devotion, or pure unconditional love. The true beauty of such a prayer is that it not only benefits the person being prayed for, but also benefits the person that is praying. Even though he or she is not looking to benefit personally from that prayer, it happens anyway. So while unconditional prayer certainly helps to improve the condition of someone else's life, it also allows God's light and grace to penetrate our *own* hearts.

I also saw how prayer helps to activate and unleash an invisible force into the world that is often beyond the ken of normal human understanding. Not only does prayer invoke God's grace and intervention into our lives, but it also helps us get closer to the Source. In fact, "miracles" or phenomena that we cannot explain away with science, logic or rational thought, are often the direct result of such interventions through prayer. Miracles are, indeed, visible proof of God's hand at play in our lives.

Remarkably, I also discovered that when lights of varying degrees of brightness come together as one in prayer — as in the case of group or congregational prayers, something quite extraordinary starts to unfold. The light in the hearts of those present seems to charge up and shine brighter, as it begins to swirl around and mingle with the other 'lights' present in the group. Amazingly, the combined power and radiance of this light helps to stoke up and rekindle the lesser 'lights' in the group. The end result is a powerful flare of light — like an SOS signal, which carries a greater thrust and momentum that has a better chance of being seen and acknowledged.

This obvious bombardment of light upon my person suddenly began to make perfect sense. I now realized that I was at the receiving end of a great deluge of prayers pouring into the heavens for my recovery. But not only was I being touched to the core, I seemed to be responding with a few sparks of my own as this magnificent outpouring of light began to converge onto every particle of my being. It was like being struck by lightning many times over, as several mega-watts of high voltage energy charged unerringly through the core and centre of my being.

Up until now the dominant colors in my immediate surroundings were a serene blue, interspersed here and there with splashes of vibrant green. I now found myself being transformed into a 'golden white' mass of living energy. I intuitively recognized this animated charge of energy as being God's gift of 'life' to me — one that had literally 'jump-started' me back to life.

At the same time, I became aware of a luminous object floating towards me in the distance that was placed squarely into the palm of my electrically-charged hand. To my great surprise it was a golden fountain pen. The 'pen,' it was impressed upon my mind, was a symbolic reminder of the 'mission' that I was to carry back with me to Earth. Just as I began to grasp the real significance of the pen as being an instrument of 'knowledge,' I found myself being draped in a scintillating fusion of liquid green light. This veneer of kaleidoscopic green seemed to somehow convey to me the gift of 'good health' that was now being bestowed upon me for my physical recovery.

* * *

Witnessing such sublime wonders of the spirit world made me realize that what I was experiencing was, indeed, unique and magical. I knew then as a matter of the deepest conviction in my heart, as well as direct personal experience, that there truly existed a higher realm of reality — one that was *not* dependent on desire or thought for its existence. Yet, it was something that the vast majority of us are not aware of.

Just as there are degrees of higher learning in our academic world, I discovered that there is a hierarchy in the spirit world that builds upon itself. Like overlapping concentric circles, each dimension both connects as well as separates one dimension from the next. And, at death, we tend to naturally gravitate towards that dimension — or plane of existence, that is most attuned to our dominant consciousness *in life*. This includes our primary beliefs, attitudes and value systems that have not only helped shape our thinking, but ultimately governed our *actions* on Earth.

Therefore, in order to gain access to a higher dimension than the one that we are currently in, we have to dramatically shift our thinking, our primary beliefs and attitudes. But it is not a matter of making a lateral shift in our thinking — namely, accumulating more of the *same* type of thoughts, but a 'paradigm' shift in our consciousness. In other words, we need to embrace an altogether *different* type of thinking which, in all likelihood, would also require a certain leap of faith on our part.

At the very least, I recognized that we needed to be open to the *possibility* that a higher reality could well exist by cultivating an openness in our thinking and thinking 'outside the box' while we were still physically alive on this earth. For, at death, our consciousness automatically zeroes in onto that dimension which meshes in with our *current* thinking.

The higher fifth dimension, I discovered, is a place that is reserved strictly for those of a more esoteric turn of mind. It draws out seekers of truth who have not only actively sought the truth, but attempted to delve into the more hidden dimensions of their lives during their time on earth. Thus, access into the fifth dimension requires a deeper kind of faith — the kind that transcends the apparent, and looks *beyond* the superficial differences of color, race, class, religion or creed, and recognizes the underlying humanity of *all* people alike.

Indeed, it struck me that it was not a 'coincidence' that I

had encountered a particular breed of individuals such as Mahatma Gandhi, Martin Luther King, Jr., and others like them on the fifth dimension. They were clearly individuals on a mission who, in their own way, had actively fought against social injustice and ingrained prejudices in the world. Above all, they were people who had stood for truth and justice for all of humankind.

In retrospect, I realized that all the individuals in the group had shared one thing in common. They were all living examples of people who had advocated the principle of 'unity in diversity.' Rather than look to differences that separate, they had looked to ties that bind. They recognized the innate equality of all people alike, and had tried to cultivate a sense of *unity consciousness* amongst all men. They had thought strictly in terms of the essential brotherhood of men, as they urged everyone to live like brothers and sisters unto each other. Martin Luther King, Jr., said it best: *"We must all learn to live together as brothers or we will all perish together as fools. We are tied together in the single garment of destiny ..."*

I discovered that what locks us into that lower fourth dimension — the dimension that is immediately adjacent to our physical third dimensional world of matter, is the nature of our thoughts, particularly our notions of "separateness." Only when we are able to see clear through our illusions of separation, and come together as one in the common spirit of brotherhood, can we hope to move forward and reach that ultimate place of Oneness.

Looking at it another way, separateness is diametrically opposed to the intrinsic unity of Oneness. Unless we are able to demonstrably shift our thinking out of its present mode of separation, and come together as one common body of humanity in *life*, we cannot hope to experience that Oneness of spirit in *death*. Thus, only when we are able to think *beyond* our superficial barriers of color, race, class, religion or creed, and think more in terms of the ONE race of people — the human race — can we hope to break through into the non-denominational domain of the fifth dimension.

* * *

Despite the thrill of being able to see from a purely fifth-dimensional perspective, I felt a little disappointed. In my heart of hearts I had expected more. In spite of being exposed to the fascinating worlds of the fourth and fifth dimensions, I was beginning to feel restless and somewhat "trapped" in my present environment. I yearned to make contact with something real and more reassuring like my Lord — not as a hidden or invisible presence, but someone that I could see in living color.

Even before I finished formulating the thought in my mind, I could hear a deep rumble of laughter in the distance which prompted me to look to the far horizon. What I witnessed next completely blew me away. In that wild and earth-shattering moment of cognizance, I knew beyond a shadow of a doubt that there was much more to heaven than I could possibly have imagined.

Immediately ahead was a broad beam of light that was

beginning to descend slowly downwards and fuse with the upper stratosphere of space directly above me. Then from within that solitary ray of brilliance, I saw several of God's Messengers begin to manifest themselves before me in all their shining glory.

As I watched in stunned silence, I realized that I was once again witnessing a 'powered down' version of these illuminated beings of light. Yet, this august body of individuals now before me somehow seemed more radiant, more vibrant, and more translucent than those in my previous group. At the same time, they appeared less dense and much less defined. It was a case of where less was definitely more.

Although I 'saw' these individuals whose particular countenance seemed familiar to me, I could not quite make out the coloring of their complexion, the color of their eyes, or the color of their hair. Instead, I saw in the purer perspective of light and shade where the very notion of color seemed superficial. The only thing that vaguely resembled color was a faint bluish-gray tint that lent a distinctly ethereal quality to their diaphanous forms. It seemed to allude to the fact that they belonged to a totally *different* plane of reality, where the notion of color or form was no longer of the essence.

What was amazing about the individuals in the present group was that they were all completely immersed in light. They were projecting themselves out of a *single* ray of light — as opposed to a series of separate and distinct lights, suggesting a lesser degree of separation from that one light Source, God. Although I could feel the glowing presence of several radiant beings of light *within the light*, I could only identify seven.

Trailing all the way to the back was the lone and bearded figure of the Prophet Noah. The rest seemed to follow in pairs. The first pair to emerge in my direct line of vision was the duskier form of the Prophet Moses, besides the more diminutive frame of Jesus Christ. They were immediately followed by a cross-legged Buddha, seated next to a flute-playing Krishna.

What struck me as a little odd at this point was the fact that I could also see a hazy, blue-toned vision of a four-armed East Indian deity projecting itself out of the slender and more effeminate frame of Lord Krishna. Their faces seemed to get a little out of focus even as they blurred into each other. It was like seeing double — except that each 'double' appeared to have a distinctly different face. I had no idea as to the identity of the four-armed deity at the time. It was not until several months later that I discovered it was *Lord Vishnu* — the East Indian deity believed to be a former reincarnation, or *avatar*, of Lord Krishna himself.

At the end of this long procession of individuals was the broad and stalwart figure of the Prophet Muhammad. Even though I have yet to see a picture or reasonable facsimile of the Prophet Muhammad, I seemed to somehow intuitively recognize him. He had a mass of thick dark hair, fair skin, and a thoughtful and penetrating quality to his eyes, something that was confirmed by his cousin and son-in-law, Hazrat Ali, in a documented description of the holy Prophet.

What surprised me, however, was the fact that standing next to the Prophet Muhammad was the shining countenance of the Virgin Mary, or *Bibi Miriam* as she is commonly referred to in Islam. Looking at it logically, I would have expected to see the figure of Mother Mary beside her son, Jesus of Nazareth. But as I found out many months later, the Virgin Mary is venerated in her own right by Muslims the world over. In fact, she merits a special place in the *Qur'an* — the Holy Book of Muslims, universally acclaimed by Muslims to be the word of God transmitted through his last Prophet, Muhammad.

As I reflected in awe upon this rare and majestic vision of the illuminated Messengers of God, I felt my spirit soar. Projecting out from the dazzling form of the Prophet Muhammad — the last in God's great line of prophets, was the luminous face of my Beloved Lord, *Ali*. I felt myself being irresistibly drawn towards their combined radiance. As I drew closer, their faces seemed to blur and become obliterated by the sheer power and brilliance of their light. All I could see was the glowing incandescence of their shining frames as they once again merged and coalesced into a *single* ray of Light. In that brief but glorious moment of illumination, I knew I had arrived. I had arrived at the very threshold of my Truth.

* * *

As I stood there dazed, it slowly sank in that I had stood in the presence of true greatness. I slowly began to grasp how each of these illuminated Messengers of God was really a different manifestation of the *same* Light. Each had not only experienced God during his or her lifetime, but also become

one with His Light for all eternity. And despite their unique-
ness — like the five fingers on my hand, I saw how each was a
legitimate instrument of God's light on Earth sent to guide
humanity along a certain path — the path of Truth.

I recognized that they were truly some of the most revered
teachers of our times, who had tried to bring a basic understanding of right and wrong, as well as ethics and morality to
the people according to the comprehension of their times.
They had, through different dialects, tried to raise a common
consciousness of the *one* God and create a greater awareness
of the eternal kingdom of God. And I now saw how each one
of them was inextricably bound to the *single* banner of God's
Light until the Day of Judgment, or the Last Day.

The Last Day, I discovered, was indeed a pre-ordained
reality — something that mankind was going to have to
reckon with some day, whether they chose to believe in it or
not. And as if to implicitly drive the point home to me, I was
briefly shown a futuristic vision of the planet Earth being
pulverized into dust and going up in a great big plume of
smoke. The closest thing that resembled it was the bombing
of Pearl Harbor during the Second World War and, more
recently, the crumbling image of the World Trade Towers in
September 2001, but on a vastly magnified scale.

It served to clearly impress upon my mind that all things
physical, *without exception* — including the planet Earth itself,
are temporal and by their very nature subject to deterioration
and destruction. The only substance that truly endures and
lives on forever is the *spirit*. To help me grasp this truth more
fully, I was also shown what appeared to be a faraway vision
of an ethereal City of Light that shimmered softly in the

distance. It was bathed in a soft golden glow of light where everything in it seemed to be fashioned out of light. It was not a reflected type of light like that of the moon, but a self-generating light like the sun that seemed to emanate from deep within itself.

The City glowed and sparkled in the distance, exuding an aura of peace and tranquility that beckoned me compellingly into its fold. Compared to the stark image of an exploding Earth, it appeared almost surreal and illusory like a mirage. Yet, it was a welcome oasis in my mind — something that seemed to exist alongside my vision of the barren desert of a crumbling Earth. Its luminous boundaries stood out to me like the gleaming jewel of God's precious truth that had managed to withstand the test of time. Indeed, to my inner eyes it was a shining symbol of God's love and everlasting peace.

* * *

The grandeur and majesty of this image swiftly drove home to me the vital distinction between what is temporal, and that which is truly eternal. And it suddenly dawned on me that the illuminated Messengers of God, too, had exuded the *same* kind of exquisite light as my City of Light. In fact, their lofty presence on the fifth dimension of more defined form now struck me as strangely incongruous. Their very *descent* into a lower dimension seemed to allude to the existence of an even higher realm of existence or reality than the one I was currently in.

Their glowing presence, along with the ephemeral vision of my City of Light, forced me to focus and set my sight steadfastly on the Truth. It made me realize that without an awareness of something finer and more exalted existing beyond our present state of consciousness, there can be no striving — only a feeling of self-complacent pride that can serve to inadvertently lock us into a dimensional rut.

The notion of 'pride' made me realize that the ego — or that part of ourselves that gives us a heightened sense of self, is still evident and very much at large even on the higher fifth-dimensional plane of existence. As I silently toyed with the notion of a hardy and indefatigable ego that continued to persist at death, I had the sudden urge to let go of all my self-centered impulses and emotions still lingering in my subconscious and directly feeding my ego.

In that single moment of honest reflection, I knew that I still had one more bridge to cross. I had to overcome the stumbling block of my emotions and own unrelenting ego, *before* I could hope to reach that final sanctuary of peace, light and love.

CHAPTER FIVE

The Emotional Self

As images flashed randomly through my mind, I found myself reliving moments of intense emotional highs and lows from my many lives lived on Earth. I was both male and female, an agnostic, a God-fearing Christian, Hindu, Muslim, Buddhist and a Jew ...

*A*s I made this profoundly unsettling realization about myself, I found myself being swallowed into a great sea of semi-gray darkness. When I came to, I felt like I had somehow lived through two separate and distinct realities *at the same time*. Along with the 'life review' and other revelations on the fifth dimension, I felt like I had simultaneously undergone an 'emotional clearing' — or a thorough airing and cleansing of all the negative emotions in my life.

Consequently, I did not exactly find myself in 'nirvana' — or that sublime state of 'nothingness,' but instead found myself suspended between two dimensions and strategically stationed outside what appeared to be yet another realm of reality. Alone and bewildered and left to my own devices in this vast wilderness of space and no-man's land once again, I found myself visiting the full spectrum of my emotions in slow and carefully modulated motion.

It was like taking a mandatory 'time-out,' where I was forced to reflect upon my innermost thoughts and feelings and plumb the very depths of my soul. It was a place for self-reflection and deep introspection, and a place to fill in the blanks in my knowledge about myself. But above all, it was a place for great self-realizations and a place to awaken to some hard-core truths about myself.

And so, one of the first realizations that I made was that undergoing a life review, in and of itself, was meaningless. It had to be accompanied by some kind of a perspective on *what* it was that had made me act a certain way and locked me into a particular behavioral pattern in the first place. In other words, I had to first identify the root cause and source of all the irrational *emotions* and self-destructive behaviors in my life. That is, I had to get a handle on that intangible part of myself called "emotion" — one that was not only getting in the way of my better judgment, but preventing me from connecting with the truth about myself.

The whole point of a 'life review,' I gathered, was to help me assess the *effect* of my actions upon others, as well as myself, during any given lifetime. An 'emotional clearing' on the other hand, forced me to flush out and bring to the forefront of my consciousness *all* emotions — irrespective of life-time, that were *causing* me to act and behave in a certain way. Both formats were essentially different sides to the same coin, designed to work hand in hand to help me understand that vital 'cause' and 'effect' relationship of the emotions running through my life.

It soon became clear to me that I could no longer turn a blind eye to my emotions and sweep them under the carpet as I had done in the past. In order to connect with the *real* me inside, I knew that I would first have to get in touch with my feelings and allow myself to *feel* those feelings. This meant that I would have to make a conscious and deliberate effort to visit the seething 'cauldron' of my emotions — emotions that had not only landed me in hot water, but were clouding my judgment and subconsciously blocking off my access to the truth.

From what I gathered, the whole point of undergoing an 'emotional clearing' was to help me grow in my awareness of myself in a *conscious* sort of way — as opposed to uncons-ciously, with my eyes half-closed. In order to bridge that gap in my understanding of myself, and cross over to the next level of reality, I knew that I would have to ascend up my ladder of consciousness — one thought-provoking rung at a time, and awaken to some pretty astonishing truths about myself.

* * *

To my great amazement, the first shocking truth I discovered was that I no longer even looked like myself! Gone was the familiar holographic image and astral projection of myself that I had grown somewhat attached to and accustomed to seeing in the mirror. Instead, I now saw myself as a misty, larger than life *ovoid* form that resembled a slightly misshapen octopus minus its tentacles — one that seemed to change color with alarming speed.

As I surveyed myself in disbelief, it registered upon my mind somewhere that I was now in a place where the notion of defined form was virtually non-existent. It suddenly struck me that this unwieldy-looking 'thing' was nothing but a visual representation of my ego — or *emotional self*, and veritable beast of my emotions. But it did not look like a two-horned devil or some kind of fire-breathing monster — just an un-impressive-looking blob that looked rather sad and forlorn, like a lost and bewildered child driven hither and thither by impulses that it could not control.

Although I displayed no human features to speak of, I could feel myself glisten and reflect back subtle hints of color. I saw myself in several shades of pale blue, mixed in with a little gray that seemed to give way to delicate hints of purple and rose-colored amethyst around the edges. By way of comparison, I was shown earlier less-refined versions of myself. One such version revealed a bright orange streak across the top, while another seemed to be cast in a deeper shade of gray with tiny flecks of fiery-red speckled all over its surface.

It dawned on me that this chameleon-like change in my colors was really a reflection of the range and intensity of my emotions over the course of *several* lifetimes lived on earth. Each color and variation thereof seemed to convey a different emotion, where the deeper the tone, the more intense and ingrained the emotion. In fact, it now occurred to me that this 'thing' masquerading as myself was really 'me' showing off my true colors! I could literally see at a glance how I was projecting myself to the world in an 'emotional' sense. It soon became apparent to me that there was absolutely no hiding from the truth, or masking one's true feelings in this place.

The deeper shades of orange and red in earlier versions of myself seemed to hint at past egotistical tendencies in my emotional make up, as well as a smoldering anger that I had often kept suppressed. The darker shades represented my less desirable emotions — ones that I had struggled with the most, and tried to overcome during the course of my many lifetimes lived on Earth. Happily, from what I could see of myself now, I appeared much lighter and clearer, and generally more even-toned in the canvas of my emotions.

This made me realize that I was not only exhibiting emotional tendencies from a single lifetime, but emotions that had spanned *several* lifetimes. It suddenly became clear to me that my 'emotional dye' had been cast *long before* I was even born into my present life. This helped drive home the fact that, apart from being a physical and spiritual being, I was also an *emotional* being — and that exhibiting emotion was essentially a part of the dynamics of being human.

As I reflected upon myself further, I saw that this 'thing'

strutting its stuff before me and seemingly calling the shots in my life, was just an overblown bag of mixed emotions. Yet, this puffed-up mass with its array of prismatic colors seemed to have the very real ability to color my perceptions of reality. And so, not only was it a visual barometer of my feelings, but it was a powerful indicator of how far I had let my 'emotions' blind me to the truth.

I now instinctively understood what Plato, the ancient Greek philosopher (428-348 B.C.) had known all along. I could now grasp the profound wisdom embedded in one of his more notable sayings, 'Self-conquest is the greatest of all victories.' I knew exactly what he was referring to — he was referring to the 'conquest' of my *emotional self* or my own personalized Satan that lived *within* me, as opposed to outside. And I saw how this insidious creature of my emotions — one that had reared its ugly head from time to time and blindsided me with its seductive whispers of non-reason and temptation, was the *real* enemy in my life.

I now realized that in order to win the greater war on the salvation of our souls, we needed to do constant battle with *ourselves* — not some imaginary devil living outside of us. Moreover, it was something that we needed to combat on a *daily* basis by actively resisting the animal-like instincts of our lower emotions — such as anger, pride, envy, greed, lust, selfishness, hatred and bitterness, to name a few. In fact, I discovered that these were the *same* emotions that were causing us to disconnect and distance ourselves from our 'true' or higher selves, and that light within.

One of the most important realizations I made here was that this ongoing *inner* struggle to gain mastery over our lower emotions and conquer this darker side of ourselves, was what constituted the true *'jihad'* — or holy war in our lives. This meant religiously examining our inner motives, as well as outward actions, and recognizing our emotional weaknesses that made us prey to that resident 'devil' within. Hence, the holiest war that we could wage was one where we took up arms against *ourselves* — where we reprimanded or chastised ourselves for our moral indiscretions every time we failed to act according to reason or some higher ideal.

I now grasped how the whole purpose of life truly hinged around 'improving' ourselves — not only in a physical and intellectual sense, but in a moral and emotional sense. And I saw how the key to this 'self-improvement' lay in mastering our egos and subduing this shadowy side of ourselves. More-over, it was firmly impressed upon my mind that, ultimately, it was the amount of struggle and effort that we put into exorcising our personal 'demons' that would determine our rate of progress on that often steep and slippery slope of evolution.

* * *

This notion of an ongoing 'inner struggle' in our lives was not altogether new to me. It was something that I had been consciously aware of since I was about thirteen years old. What I did not know, however, was that the passion and emotion that fed and stoked our egos was also a major driving force in our lives. Not only did it have the potential of getting us into hot water, but it also had the real power to drive us forward. In other words, our emotions acted like a double-edged sword that could either make us or break us, depending on just how well we were able to control this brute force of our emotions.

It now became very clear to me that we are, indeed, 'emotionally' driven beings. To stifle that passion or emotion from our lives completely would be to turn ourselves into robots or emotionless zombies. Just as the breaking in of a wild horse or animal requires the firm hand of his master's touch, similarly, what is required here is the firm handling of our emotions and taming them into subservience. So what matters, in the final analysis, is how well we are able to harness this animal-like force of our emotions to serve us better — both as individuals and society as a whole.

One of our main tasks as human beings is to transform and direct the raw power of our passions and emotions into a more constructive force in our lives. The goal is to make it work for us rather than against us. This requires a 'balanced' or controlled approach to life. It means injecting just the 'right mix' of spontaneous emotion and disciplined restraint into our work-a-day lives. It also means knowing exactly when to slam the brakes, and when to accelerate down the speed-way of our lives. Finally, it requires that we keep a tight leash on this passionate and impulsive part of ourselves by exer-cising the right amount of caution, and intellectual restraint, over this highly volatile aspect of ourselves.

God's greatest gift to mankind is his intellect — one that distinguishes His finest creation man, from the beast.

And it is our very ability to think, reason and ultimately differentiate between right and wrong, that enables us to keep this unruly 'animal' side of ourselves in check. It is primarily through the use of our intellects that we are able to restrain ourselves and find that higher moral ground in our lives. Our intellect, therefore, remains our most powerful weapon for keeping our ego and emotions at bay.

During those times when we are blinded to the truth by our emotions and foolish egos, and are unable to draw upon our intellect and the wisdom of that 'inner voice of reason,' all is not lost. We can always look to the wisdom, example and moral teaching of others — such as the great prophets or messengers of God, and moralists of our time, who walked the Earth before us.

Their main purpose was to remind us of the truth that we once knew but have since forgotten by introducing a certain degree of morality into our lives. Even though their teachings later evolved into separate 'religions' with a distinct linguistic flavor, they essentially taught the *same* thing. All monotheistic faiths, in essence, center round the same fundamental premise of belief in the one God and principles of universal conduct and ethical behavior.

While all organized religions try to provide an outer framework for worship, the true essence or inner core of *all* religions revolves around the same thing — namely, the call to lead more moral lives. Thus, every time we make a genuine effort to lead morally upright and ethical lives, we are in essence improving upon our character and the *inner* condition of our spirit. And every time we try to improve upon our character and the inner condition of our *spirit*, we are in effect practicing '*spirituality*' — which is the true intent and purpose of *all* religions, regardless of their founder.

As the ancient Greek philosopher Socrates wisely pointed out, what is important is not living, but living *rightfully*. Therefore, until such time as we are able to have an honest and open dialogue with our own inner voice of conscience — one that prompts us to live morally upright and ethical lives, we need to look *outside* ourselves. We can look to the religious commandments, as well as the wisdom and moral teachings of those more enlightened amongst us.

* * *

Before I could consider the importance of personal integrity, ethics, or right and wrong in my life, I knew that I would have to pinpoint and narrow in on those emotions that were making me act unconscionably in the first place. In the wake of this powerful realization, I could feel the dense mists of my forgetfulness begin to lift and slowly disperse from within the inner recesses of my mind. Then, incredibly, there stretched out before me along the vast expanse of eternity were several of my personalities from the past.

As images flashed randomly through my mind, I could feel the first stirring of emotion enter my heart. Before long, I found myself reliving moments of intense emotional highs and lows from my many lives lived on earth. What seemed remarkable was the fact that even though I only saw snippets from those lives, I was able to recognize the full thrust and essence of any given lifetime simply by the intensity of emotion that welled up inside of me. As flashback after flashback let loose a thousand fluttering feelings upon my heart, speaking volumes to my soul, I made a vital discovery. I realized that how I *felt* — whether it was good, bad or indifferent — was how my soul tried to communicate with me. Emotion, I discovered, is truly the language of the soul.

The lives that surfaced seemed to run the gamut. I was a living paradox of contrasting emotions that crossed the barriers of time and space, as well as color, race, class, sex, religion or creed. I was both male and female, primitive and sophisticated, literate and illiterate, an agnostic, a devout Muslim, a God-fearing Christian, Hindu, Buddhist and a Jew, who had literally lived all over the world.

Among my more memorable lives, I recalled a lifetime as royalty and a blue-blooded female living in Scotland with a deep passion for horses, as well as one as an impoverished poacher in England. There were others, such as a peasant woman living in France during the French Revolution, a free-spirited Spanish gypsy woman, Jewish widow, Quaker child, Franciscan monk, sweetmeat merchant in India, paddy field worker in communist China, a Roman soldier, as well as a gun-toting bandit to name a few. One that seemed particularly poignant was a lifetime in captivity as a black slave where I saw myself being taken in chains from the West Coast of Africa. I also recalled another lifetime as a slave in ancient Egypt during the building of the pyramids, where I saw myself get crushed beneath a giant slab of stone.

What stood out for me particularly, however, were my past life connections with my father and 'Uncle Val' — namely, Chief Justice Milvain, whose biography I had just recently published. As I recall, both these individuals had been present during my meeting with the Council of Elders. Now they also appeared to be individuals with whom I had forged strong emotional ties in former lifetimes. I could vividly recollect two lifetimes with each.

I clearly recalled life as a primitive savage with my father in Australia, at a time when it was still a part of the now sub-merged continental shelf that extends along the northern coast of Australia. It was also my *first* life as a soul taking on the human experience. In another lifetime with my father, I remember seeing myself as a blind and orphaned youth trying to survive the harsh reality of life as a newly-arrived immigrant in the 'New World' of America.

It appeared that my father had always played the role of a disciplinarian in my life. He had tried to instill in me the value of self-discipline and, among other things, tried to teach me right from wrong. Even though I always felt a little fearful and in awe of him, occasionally even balking at his authority over me, I nevertheless shared an arm's length relationship with him that still remained very evident. But it was not the same kind of emotional closeness that I shared with my mother who, incidentally, had also been my mother in a previous lifetime.

As far as 'Uncle Val' was concerned, I was surprised to learn that I had actually shared a past life connection with him, despite the fact I did not have a real 'blood' connection with him in my most recent life. And for some reason the emotions that surfaced seemed almost more intense than those that I had shared with my father. I felt an overwhelming affection for the man that I called Uncle Val.

From what I saw of my past life connections with Uncle Val, it appeared that in an earlier lifetime we had shared a strong spiritual bond as Tibetan monks. He was my Master and I was his pupil, and I could distinctly recall him teaching me the art of one-pointed meditation using a lighted candle as a prop. In another lifetime together as Native American Indians, he had been a respected elder and medicine man who possessed a vast knowledge of natural herbs and healing. He was also my grandfather in that lifetime.

In all my life experiences with Uncle Val, it appeared that he had always played the role of a teacher and mentor who had, in one way or another, helped shape me into the person that I had become. As a result, I always felt a deep sense of gratitude towards him that had carried over into my present life. Although it was not something that I was conscious of, it had nevertheless manifested itself as an overpowering compulsion to repay him for his past kindness to me. This had in turn led me to actively research and document his life. In the process, I had managed to absolve myself from a huge debt of gratitude that I felt I owed him without actually having been aware of it.

* * *

In that moment of expanded awareness, it suddenly dawned on me that the source of my *present* emotions was not necessarily rooted in early childhood. More often than not, it was a carryover from *previous* lifetimes. And I saw how the 'snowballing' effect of my emotions had the ability to literally put me in bondage, life after life after life. And until such time as I was able to discharge those negative emotions still festering in my system, I knew I would continue to return to Earth time and time again and, in all likelihood, once again take on the human form.

I now saw how many of the more painful emotions in my life — whether from childhood or *beyond,* had the tendency to gather momentum and get rapidly out of control if left unchecked. Then before I knew it, the tiny polyp of my emotion had grown into a full-blown cancer — totally out of proportion to the original emotion. Like a cancer eating away at my soul, I knew that I would have to actively seek out and eradicate those malignant emotions that had already taken root in my soul to prevent the cancer from spreading further.

Life in the final analysis, I realized, is a matter of *cleaning up our acts.* It is a matter of working through the dense quagmire of our less desirable emotions like anger, lust, envy, greed, hatred, pride and bitterness, among others. Just like a spill of crude oil that floats on top of a pristine ocean, I discovered that our negative emotions, too, have a tendency to settle on the surface of our soul like a heavy sludge. The more intense and embedded the emotion, the darker and more resistant this layer of sludge, and the greater the number of lifetimes of struggle and effort that would be required to disperse it.

Yet, one thing remained abundantly clear — the layer of sludge or 'emotional dirt' would always remain a *separate* entity from my soul. The superficial veneer of sludge could never become a part of the finer and clearer waters of my soul beneath, as the twain — water and oil — could never mix. Therefore, one thing I knew, one way or another I would have to clean up the toxic emotions in my system, somewhere during the course of my many lifetimes on Earth.

Looking at it another way, our 'emotional self' acts as a virtual dumping ground for the excesses of emotion carried over from both our present as well as previous lifetimes. So before we can hope to catch a tiny glimpse of our 'true' selves lying beneath the junk pile of our emotions, we need to first off-load some of that 'emotional baggage' from our systems. But like trying to lose weight, it is something that we have to personally work on ourselves. This means we have to literally 'starve' the fat cells of our negative emotions by exercising some measure of restraint or self-control in our lives, by not giving in to our 'emotional' cravings.

We can also work off any accumulated reserves of negative emotion by 'walking through' those emotions and facing them head on. This means that we can no longer anaesthetize or suppress our emotional pain by using whatever short-term 'fix' we deem appropriate — whether in the form of food, alcohol or drugs. Using mood-altering substances or engaging in self-destructive behaviors may help to *temporarily* numb the pain and emptiness inside, but it also tends to severely cloud our judgment — which further compromises our ability to *think* and, therefore, act rationally.

Furthermore, by engaging in substance abuse to help cope with the pain inside by *suppressing* our emotions, we are, in fact, compounding the very problem that we are trying to work through in the first place. We are distancing ourselves from our *emotions* — the very thing that is subconsciously triggering off our impulsive behaviors. But before we can begin to neutralize our negative emotions, we need to first *acknowledge* those emotions. In other words, we have to deliberately and consciously confront those emotional 'demons' that may have insinuated themselves into our lives — whether in the form of anger, rage, envy, pride, greed, lust or whatever else.

* * *

Emotions in and of themselves are healthy. It is only when they start to get out of hand and negatively impact our lives that we start running into problems. I was once again reminded that one way of preventing this wayward beast of our emotions from gaining the upper hand in our lives, was through the use of our 'intellect' — the one thing that set us apart from the beast.

By bringing reason and intellect to bear upon some of our irrational emotions, we theoretically have the ability to get past our emotions. In reality though, it is not quite as straight forward as that as I found myself asking the question, "*What about those emotions that were already contaminating my system and preventing me from thinking rationally in the first place?*"

I knew there was no easy way around this. The only way to penetrate the dense wall of my emotions was for me to first acknowledge my emotions, and then courageously face up to those emotions. Therefore, in order to heal myself emotionally, I would first have to clear away those toxic emotions *already* clogging up my system. This would require me to go through the painful process of 'opening up' the festering wound of my emotions — and allowing it to drain, *before* I could begin to heal myself.

One way of 'opening up' our emotional wounds, I found, was to work through the various layers of our emotions through the process called *catharsis*. By consciously applying the three R's of catharsis — namely, *Revisiting*, *Reliving* and then finally *Releasing* the negative memories associated with those emotions, we have a powerful tool in our hands with which to get rid of the emotional toxicity in our system.

In other words, by deliberately *recreating* those emotions and looking them squarely in the eye, we technically have the ability to off-load our emotions and release ourselves from the gross errors in judgment associated with those emotions. Looking at it another way, our pent-up emotions act like a 'tarnish' upon the clear mirror of our soul that creates a distinct fuzziness and distortion in our perception of reality. As the 18th century poet and mystic, William Blake, wisely pointed out: "*If the doors of perception are cleansed everything would appear to man as it is, Infinite. For man has closed himself up till he sees all things thro' narrow chinks of his cavern.*"

Thus, in order for us to evolve to a higher state of con-sciousness and recognize the 'Infinite' in our lives, cleansing our *doors of perception* by getting rid of the baser emotions that distort our reality then becomes an essential step in our evolution. Getting in touch with our true feelings, however, is a slow and painful process that requires that we be brutally honest with ourselves. It requires a critical self-examination of ourselves where we have to reflect upon both our inner motives, as well as outward actions, and subject ourselves to a thorough psychoanalysis — either privately, if we are capable of being totally honest, or professionally, if we are not.

Unless we are willing to take a good look in the mirror and confront the truth about ourselves — our fears, our nega-tivity, and our own role in creating our problems, we cannot lay our pasts to rest and heal ourselves emotionally. Yet, once we stop identifying with our ego, or 'emotional self,' and recognize that we are *more than the sum total of our feelings*, we have the very real ability to move forward and connect with that true and authentic part of ourselves just waiting to be discovered.

* * *

Life in the final analysis is a matter of identifying with the truth and making peace with ourselves, God, and our fellow man. There can be no lasting peace in our lives if we allowed the memory of our past hurts, mistakes, errors and omissions to continuously impinge upon our present life. As human beings we have an inherent need for closure. But until such time as we are willing to 'let go' of our grievances by showing a certain level of emotional maturity and integrity in our lives, we will never achieve the peace that we so deeply crave.

This means taking ownership of the problems in our lives and taking responsibility for our *own* emotional shortcomings — of anger, pride, envy, hatred, greed or whatever else, before pointing a finger of blame at others. It means letting go of all our fears, our obsessions and the negativity in our lives. This requires that we actively seek forgiveness for the harm that we may have caused others — whether it was intentional or unintentional.

'Letting go' also means forgiving those who may have willfully or intentionally harmed us in some way by recognizing the greater wisdom of God's will in our lives. But more than anything else, I was reminded that forgiveness was a 'choice' and that *we ourselves were forgiven only to the extent that we were able to forgive others.*

In being reminded of this ancient piece of wisdom, I realized that by letting go, we actually helped *ourselves* far more than those we forgave. Incredibly, we have the very real ability to release ourselves from our past hatreds, bitterness and other grievances, through that single act of forgiveness.

Moreover, forgiveness not only helps to stamp out the cancer in our soul, but it helps heal those emotional wounds that may be holding us back in our lives. Logically, we cannot move forward if we are still holding too rigidly to our past. Therefore, 'forgiveness' and 'letting go' as such go hand in hand to help us move genuinely forward in our lives and the evolutionary journey of our souls.

Another way of finding some measure of peace in our lives, I was reminded, was to also *act upon* our more positive emotions. Every time we acted on some noble impulse, and demonstrated a spirit of kindness or generosity in the form of compassion, love or selfless service, we were, in effect, invoking God's grace and benevolence into our own lives.

Thus, every time we gave of ourselves to others in some small gesture of kindness, charity, generosity or service, we were clearing a direct path towards God. Remarkably, it dawned on me that by acting upon our more noble impulses, we were not only reflecting attributes worthy of the Divine, but we were, in actual fact, revealing a tiny glimpse of our *own* divine natures in the process!

* * *

In making this startling discovery and thought-provoking truth about myself, I realized that by squashing some of my negative emotions and, *at the same time*, acting upon my more positive impulses, I had found the elusive key with which to slowly but surely free myself from those confining chains of reincarnation — or repeated lifetimes on earth.

Even as this realization sank in, I could feel my ovoid form begin to whither and disintegrate. It was as though I had, at long last, managed to shed my emotional skin and crack open the outer shell of my emotions. I realized that, in the process of letting go, I had found myself — or the *real* me that lay trapped beneath the deadweight of my emotions.

CHAPTER SIX

City of Light

It was like being swept into a great big Ocean of Light.
I felt like a tiny leaf being tossed about in a tempestuous
sea. As I surrendered myself to the Ocean, I realized that
'I' – or that part which used to be 'me,' no longer existed
separate and apart from the almighty Ocean ...

In that sweet moment of release, I felt an exhilarating
rush of freedom. Amazingly, I had shattered the tough
and resistant casing of my ego and 'emotional self' against the
hard rock of my truth. The essential 'me' — or true essence
of who I was, had finally broken free from its moorings and
the stranglehold of my emotions.

In that flitting moment of abandon, I could feel myself
break gloriously free from the heavy fetters of my emotions

and delusions about myself. Gone was that oppressive feeling of being trapped and boxed into an existence that no longer had the power to contain or captivate me. And like a butterfly that had just earned its fragile little wings, I found myself emerge warily out of my chrysalis and burst ecstatically forth into a bright New World of light, beauty, freedom and joy.

I seemed to lose all sense of awareness of myself as light flooded my being. But at a deeper level of consciousness, I felt more alive and more aware than I ever remember being. All my sensibilities seemed to somehow reach out to me from *beyond* the boundary of my disintegrated form. Then inexplicably, out of the blue, I noticed a dazzling whirl of light coming directly towards me — or that part of 'me' that still remained conscious. It began to crystallize into the luminous image of what looked like an old man. But as it drew closer, I realized with a start that this swirling mass of radiant energy was none other than myself!

I had literally come face to face with my 'true' or shining higher self and was seeing clear through to the light of my own soul. It was like catching a rare glimpse of myself, or that precious part of me that had always lain dormant beneath the heavy mantle of my emotions and illusory world of matter. It was like being united with a long lost friend. But mostly, it felt like I was marveling at the captivating brilliance of a faraway star — only to realize that the star was *me*.

In that single flash of recognition, I saw how in perceiving the truth, not only does one get closer to the truth but also *becomes* that Truth. It was like being suddenly metamorphosized into this beautiful white light that easily outshone and surpassed my wildest expectations of myself. It was as though after enduring eons of compression as a lowly and humble piece of coal, I had been transformed into an unpolished diamond in the rough, only to realize my true destiny as the brilliant solitaire that I was.

In the process of discovering my 'true' self — or that radiant part of me that had always been there since the beginning of time, I found myself rapidly becoming privy to truths that I could not quite fathom before. I could now instantly grasp the immutable and self-evident truths about reincarnation, personal accountability and karmic retribution. And I saw how the whole point of life, and repeated lifetimes on Earth, was to make each one of us aware and personally accountable for our actions in life so that, in the process, we could reform ourselves.

As diamonds in the rough, I realized that our task on Earth was to buff ourselves to perfection against those hard and gritty challenges in life. In fact, the very act of enduring or struggling to overcome those painful trials and tribulations in our lives provided that abrasive polish against which to slough-off the moral dirt embedded in the innermost reaches of our soul. Thus, life on Earth, I discovered, was a matter of getting rid of our moral impurities in order to bring out the true beauty and inner brilliance of our souls.

I now understood, not ideologically or hypothetically — but with my heart and soul, the clear and irrefutable truth about reincarnation. I could see how the many bodies that I had assumed life after life, were just superficial masks or vehicles that I had utilized in order to exist in an environment of dense physical matter to improve upon myself. But like a fine wine, this process of 'improvement' and full-bodied maturity took time and infinite patience. It was delusional on our part to think that we, as ordinary human beings, could eliminate *all* our character flaws and defects and achieve perfection in the course of a *single* lifetime.

Yet, from the perspective of the soul a single lifetime amounts to but the blink of an eye, compared to the timeless span of eternity now before me. And as if to lend validity to this awe-inspiring truth, I found myself looking upon the vast vista of eternity from the standpoint of my own light. All the various personalities that I had donned on in previous lifetimes were now paraded before me like shadowy apparitions in the night. Compared to the real and substantive light of my soul, it was like catching a hazy reflection of my many selves upon the smooth and tranquil surface of a ripple-free pond.

In seeing myself being reflected back as several distinct personalities from my past, I realized that there was, indeed, only ONE actor acting out the different roles and exploring different aspects of myself. In the process of discovering my *real* self, I was able to recognize the perpetuity of my own soul. And I saw how the real mover and shaker behind all my changing faces was the *same* one that had endured and perpetuated itself throughout eternity.

* * *

Facing the truth has a way of setting you free from your constraints of inner vision and illusions about yourself. In catching a tiny glimpse of the light of my own soul, all the lingering shadows of doubt and darkness began to magically vanish from my mind. Suddenly, I found myself looking at the full spectrum of my life as a soul from a much higher and grander perspective than I could have imagined was possible.

I now understood the fundamental truth about life on Earth. I saw the true condition of our souls — one that is without beginning or end, and how at the end of the day all our lives simply rolled into one. I also saw how each segment that we call a 'lifetime' is really a unique learning experience and incursion into physical life, one that not only consolidates the lessons learned, but provides a framework upon which further learning can take place.

I could now grasp how every end is followed by a new beginning, and how each of our strife-filled lives on earth is really a means to an end, and *not* an end in itself. I also saw how each lifetime is an act of immense physical and spiritual courage, undertaken specifically for the purpose of *improving* upon ourselves and finally breaking free from the chains of reincarnation — or repeated lifetimes on earth.

What makes us typically earthbound, life after life, is our lack of moral integrity, our emotional shortcomings, and those weaknesses in our character. In order to be truly free, we need to return to our home in God, from whence we came, in a much improved and 'enlightened' condition than when we first left as infantile little sparks of light. Much like the return of the prodigal son, we have to come full circle. We have to ultimately return Home from our travels on Earth — reformed, and much the wiser for wear, than when we first set out as tiny fragments of light.

But in order for our fledgling souls to finally return to Source, we need to do it as *spirit* — at the pure and intrinsic level of *light* or energy that goes beyond color, feature or form. In fact, it occurred to me that at the level of 'light,' the true measure of one's growth and maturity as souls was really the amount of *light* we were able to reflect back from ourselves. In other words, what mattered here was how brightly our individual star could shine. Indeed, ultimately it is the condition of this inner *light* in us — or our particular state of 'enlightenment' — that would determine the grace and timing of our final merger with the greater Light of God.

Discovering one's own light is, therefore, the single most defining moment in the life of an individual soul. For me, it was that first real step towards my sanctuary of Light and peace. It is only through the clear recognition of this inner light — or the spark of divine in us, that access into the sixth dimension is gained.

* * *

Seeing my own light was like seeing the breaking of dawn before the full sunrise of my life. Although I was not yet fully into the heart of the sixth dimension, I had at least managed to get my foot in the door. And like a quivering arrow on the verge of breaking through into the next dimension, I found myself poised and ready for take-off on the outermost edge of the sixth dimension.

Surprisingly enough, it seemed darker here on the edge of the sixth dimension. But it was not an inky darkness, the kind that one associated with hell, but a soft translucent darkness that seemed more blue than black. It slowly sank in that in a dimension of formless reality such as this, where the notion of color or form was practically non-existent, you 'saw' in the purer perspective of light and shade. Consequently, I realized that some measure of darkness was actually necessary here in order for me to see and recognize my *own* light. In fact, it was enabling me to cast my own light onto the strangely violet skies.

The backdrop of purple and indigo skies seemed to lend an almost regal and dignified air to the surroundings. It also helped define and accentuate the other lights in the sky. I soon realized that I was not alone and that mine was not the only light illuminating the sky. I could see other 'lights' silhouetted against the dusky velvet skies, huddled together in the distance in clusters of solid light.

It was like looking at clumps of white-hot coal. Some seemed inert and barely there, while others were alive and fully aglow. Although I could not distinguish the individual lights within the clusters, I seemed to recognize the unit as a whole. Strangely enough, this recognition came not at the level of feature or form — which did not exist anyway, but rather at the level of their aggregate brightness. In other words, I could only identify with the individual lights in the unit by the amount of *cumulative* light that they reflected.

It struck me that birds of a feather certainly flocked together, which seemed to be especially the case here. I noted a greater sense of cohesiveness here than I had anywhere else.

The emphasis here seemed to be on functioning as a unit, on 'unity consciousness' and togetherness — as opposed to division and separation. I also discerned a palpable emotion here, one that acted as a powerful glue that held everything together. It was the unmistakable emotion of *unconditional love* — one that not only transcended matter and our lower emotions, but thought itself. I realized that I was now *beyond* thought.

Just then, an explosion of pure feeling overwhelmed my being as I made another mind-blowing discovery. Truth in the higher planes of reality is *felt*, as opposed to rationally understood. It is something that is *experienced* at the level of the soul and is that elusive X factor which adds the necessary element of conviction to our hearts.

I was once again reminded that the medium of expression here was through the vehicle of our emotions. Moreover, I discovered that the truth on the higher dimensions is conveyed primarily through our *higher* and positive emotions — namely, our emotions of love, compassion, mercy, generosity and gratitude to name a few. I further learned that these emotions do not only resonate and vibrate at the higher frequency of the sixth dimension, but they form an intrinsic part of the fabric of the soul itself.

On the other hand, our lower vibrating emotions of envy, pride, anger, greed, lust, hatred and selfishness — ones that we need to actively combat and overcome *before* we can gain access into the sixth dimension — exist only as a superficial veneer or 'tarnish' upon the clear mirrors of our soul. And, more than anything else, I saw that it is this layer of 'moral dirt' on our soul that prevents us from connecting with our inner light and that true and authentic part of ourselves just waiting to be discovered.

As I reflected upon this extraordinary truth, I found myself at center stage in what appeared to be an open-air coliseum of some sort. Incredibly, I seemed to be the main focus of love, attention, and even adulation. I could see row upon row of softly bulging lights stretched out before me like strings of luminescent pearls. Some appeared brighter than others, but the mood overall was one of supreme elation and warm jubilation. The air was electric and charged with a joy that I could almost reach out and touch. The atmosphere was vibrant and filled with an overwhelming sense of love that swept me into a great tidal wave of pure emotion.

It became apparent to me that everyone present was whole-heartedly celebrating my return. But more than celebrating my homecoming, they were rejoicing at that which I had become as a result of my sojourns on Earth.

* * *

Coming into one's own light is a grand and stupendous moment in the life of an individual. It represents the coming of age of the soul — like that wondrous moment when a bud first opens itself and sees its true potential as a flower. And it is this glorious moment of awakening that typically marks the rite of passage of a soul into the mystical sixth dimension of light and symbiotic shade.

Gaining a foothold into the sixth dimension is without a doubt an auspicious milestone in the life of a soul — and one, as I was about to discover, that is accompanied by a certain amount of ceremonial. At a physical level, it mimics the pomp and majesty of a grand and lavish wedding ceremony on Earth — complete with an eclectic display of light that heralds a new era in the life of that individual. For some reason, I even began to see myself as a *glowing bride* patiently awaiting the call to the side of her Beloved.

This was apparently my moment to shine as I found myself being prepared for an initiation ceremony of some sort amidst a great flurry of activity. Up until now, I had seen myself as a formless energy of light without color, feature or form. But as I was draped and adorned in what looked like a 'glitter suit,' I could once again visualize myself taking on the human form. Putting on this shiny one-piece garment made out of a gossamer-fine material that resembled an exquisite chain mail, helped to contain and reflect my inner light. But, more than that, it changed the way I perceived myself as it once again lent a distinctly human dimension to my soul.

I now saw myself transformed into an actualized human being. I was no longer the portly figure that I had grown into in the last decade or so of my life, but a perfectly molded androgynous form that was neither male nor distinctly female. I felt 'balanced,' complete, and at peace with myself. It appeared that in my most recent but tentative life as a female, I had managed to integrate into myself some of the more feminine aspects necessary to complement the male component already present in my repertoire of soul experiences. I now felt totally and utterly at one with myself.

Remarkably, in thinking back, I remembered that I had actually been afforded a glimpse into some of the ceremony associated with the 'glitter suit' in a dream some *twenty-six* years before. My Uncle Badur — one of the kindest and gentlest persons that I have ever known, had appeared to me in a dream wearing a 'golden' tuxedo made out of the same reflective material that I had on now. He looked positively radiant and appeared to be celebrating his joyous return to the spirit world.

Even though I did not attach any special significance to that dream at the time — other than a sign that my Uncle was alive and well in the hereafter, I could now appreciate the deeper relevance of that dream. I realized that, in retrospect, it had been a wake-up call and subtle reminder from my subconscious to help prepare me for the grandest celebration of my life — and my *own* moment in the Sun.

* * *

As an introduction to the main event, I found myself being treated to a celestial light show of breathtaking beauty that was accompanied by the delicate strains of lightly hypnotic music. It was the type of haunting melody that transcended the barriers of time, genre and place, and spoke directly to my soul. More than 'hearing' the notes, I *felt* the rhythmic rise and swell of the music as it exploded into a crashing crescendo of ecstasy inside. I could feel myself literally melt and fade into the luxuriant overtones of the musical rhapsody, as I became one with the rich symphony of sounds resonating within my soul.

And so, it was not the blare of a trumpet that heralded the start of the proceedings afoot, but the quieter and softer timbre of a harp that wove itself spellbindingly into my soul. Someone was playing a harp somewhere in the sky above me. Although I could not quite make out who it was, I got the distinct impression that it was a female form draped in a toga reminiscent of a Greek goddess. I could see other illustrious shapes begin to materialize in the skyline directly above me. This time I seemed to intuitively recognize one of the female figures to my left. It was a larger than life image of *Sita* — the legendary Hindu princess purported to be the reincarnation of *Laksmi* and consort of Lord Rama.

As I witnessed the mesmerizing play of light upon the darkly ethereal skies, I noticed several whirls of light suddenly sweep into focus at lightning speed from what appeared to be a faraway galaxy of space. They seemed to have a life of their own as they quickly arranged themselves into graceful configurations of light. The end result was the formation of several constellations of brilliant white stars that appeared almost linear in their formation — like one-line drawings in neon lights.

As I watched enthralled, the intricate formations of light began to emblazon themselves boldly against the indigo blue skies and position themselves strategically above the clusters of softer, more muted lights around the coliseum. I somehow got the impression that these strangely vivified configurations of light were here exclusively by invitation. They seemed to literally come alive for me as I began to slowly distinguish some of the glowing shapes sprawled across this vast infinity of space around me.

As I watched closely, I discovered to my great astonishment that what I was looking at were really straight-line depictions of the heads and torsos of people that I actually recognized from my history books! These 'star heads,' as I like to refer to them, seemed to symbolically convey to me that what mattered here on the sixth dimension was what was *inside* our heart, and in the space between our ears. They represented the intellectual elite and creative geniuses of our time that had spanned the ages.

One of the first shapes that I recognized was that of the ancient Greek philosopher Socrates, followed by his student Plato (whom I was only able to identify a few years later). Next to them was the imposing image of the 15th century Italian renaissance painter, Leonardo da Vinci. To their right was the distinctive outline of the 16th century English playwright, William Shakespeare, followed by the 18th century Austrian born musical genius, Beethoven. Right behind them was the more recent and recognizable face of the 20th century Nobel Prize winner and nuclear physicist, Albert Einstein — popularly regarded as the 'father of modern physics.' He was followed closely by the German theologian, philosopher, missionary and winner of the 1952 Nobel Peace Prize, Albert Schweitzer.

These 'star heads' to my mind did not only denote the academics and geniuses of our time, but individuals who came with stellar credentials. They were the trailblazers and some of the brightest stars in our universe whose light had definitely shone the brightest. They were the poets, painters, scientists, artists, musicians, philosophers, humanitarians and inspired thinkers who had helped to dramatically revolutionize the thinking of our times. They were the renaissance men, the movers and shakers of our age who had awakened us to new possibilities — both in the world around us, as well as *within* ourselves.

As I reflected upon their awe-inspiring contributions to the richness and progress of human civilization, I found myself being thrust under a powerful spotlight. It was a solid beam of light that appeared to be projected from directly overhead. It was like being immersed in an infusion of pure white light whose all-embracing brilliance was unlike anything I had known. It was as though I had suddenly emerged out of the cave of my shadowy existence and into the full-beamed brightness of the world outside.

As light permeated the very core and essence of my being, I realized that I was now out of the half-light and periphery of my consciousness, and firmly ensconced in the heart of the mystical sixth dimension. In the next instant, I found myself being beamed up and drawn into the narrowest point of this conical ray of light.

It felt like I was going through the eye of a needle as I found myself moving swiftly out of the narrow confines of my mind. I could feel the shifting sands of my consciousness begin to slowly drift *upwards* through the narrow opening of the hourglass of my mind. As realization upon realization began to heap upon my mind, the existing content of my mind began to spill itself into a vast crucible of living light. The existing content of my mind, I realized, had to be necessarily dismantled and rearranged *before* it could expand itself into the fullness of the surrounding light.

In order for me to be able to assimilate my new reality, I had to undergo a total restructuring and paradigm shift in my consciousness that resulted in a dramatic shift in my perception of reality itself. And like the delicately unfolding petals of a rare and precious flower, I began to feel the half-opened bud of my inner eye open, petal by petal, as it slowly blossomed into the full flowering of its truth. Then swiftly and effortlessly, and in the blink of an eye, the unspeakable and inherent beauty of my inner world began to come into sharper focus. I no longer had a partial or hooded view of reality, but a panoramic vision of the truth.

* * *

As I took in the breathtakingly clear and unobstructed view of my inner world, it struck me that I was now *inside* the City of Light. I appeared to be in a cavernous repository of light, filled with gem upon gem of knowledge and infinitely glowing wisdom. As I gazed into this vast treasure-house of light, it suddenly dawned on me that the *light* flooding my mind was really an energetic representation of the wisdom and knowledge illuminating this space.

In my state of heightened consciousness, I was able to see how 'wisdom' accumulated over several lifetimes is stored in the form of 'light.' And it struck me that my particular state of *enlightenment* depended entirely upon how much wisdom I had managed to accumulate during my present, as well as previous lifetimes on Earth.

It made me realize that the process of 'enlightenment' is truly an ongoing and cumulative process of evolution. It is not just a matter of possessing a superficial or theoretical knowledge that can be crammed into one's head, but it is a deeper more esoteric understanding of the truth. More often than not, it is knowledge or wisdom that has been garnered through actual life experiences — something that has to be personally *experienced* in order for it to be fully understood.

Therefore, *light*, I realized, lies at the heart of all true knowledge and wisdom in all realms of reality. Even as I tried to grasp the full essence of the light surrounding me, I began to feel increasingly like a dried-out sponge that was being systematically revived in a gigantic vat of liquid light. The light, it appeared, was not only illuminating my mind but causing an actual expansion in my consciousness. It was also chasing away the lingering shadows of doubt and ignorance from within the deepest and darkest corners of my mind.

I could feel my mind expand even more as it began to encompass images from further afield that were starting to drift into my radar of consciousness. Then out of the corner of my inner eye, I could once again see the luminous head of Albert Schweitzer loom up against my light-filled horizon. He was followed by the unmistakable face of Albert Einstein, with his shock of unruly hair and distinctive moustache.

Others, too, bobbed up into the light — like untethered balloons, but their image seemed fainter and less distinct. Whereas I had previously only seen a two-dimensional outline of their heads and upper torsos, I could now see every feature on their faces exquisitely chiseled in light from what appeared to be a uniquely multi-dimensional perspective. It was like seeing an over-exposed negative, or the embossed head on a shiny new coin. The effect was striking as light played upon endless light, in graceful little ripples of undulating light.

From my great vista of light, I could now see from the perspective of pure light — something that I could not do before. Then, out of nowhere, I again saw the image of a golden fountain pen being projected into this luminous space. It struck me that while the 'pen' was really a symbolic reminder of the 'mission' that I was to carry back with me to earth, this liquid light of knowledge in which I was immersed could one day form the very 'ink' to flow through my pen.

As I tried to grapple with the deeper relevance of the 'pen' and other symbolisms that I had encountered in the spirit world, it occurred to me that a symbol speaks to the subconscious mind and always points *beyond* itself. While the written word was my preferred mode of expression, I recognized that it was also my main avenue for disseminating knowledge. It suddenly crossed my mind that I was being enlightened by the same 'light of knowledge' as had other crusaders of truth before me. I realized that Albert Schweitzer and the other luminaries that had converged onto this space, too, had been similarly inspired. They had drawn their inspiration and creative wisdom from the *same* pool of light and divine knowledge in which I was currently steeped.

* * *

I realized with a deep and abiding sense of gratitude that to have experienced an expansion in consciousness, even to the slightest degree, was a gift from God — something that was given as opposed to being taken. It made me realize that connecting my tiny ray of consciousness to that of the all-knowing Sun was not a matter of religious privilege, or professional pride. Nor was it a matter of individual freewill choice, personal preference or evolutionary right, but purely and simply a matter of Divine grace.

I sensed, however, that in order to be able to penetrate this august kingdom of light, a certain amount of spiritual humility was also warranted. It was absolutely incumbent that we checked our egos at the door. In order to participate at the level of inspired thought, we needed to acknowledge and bow down to the power of a superior Will and Intelligence at work in our lives besides our own. In other words, we not only have to acknowledge the existence of something greater than ourselves, but also need to submit ourselves willingly to the will and agency of that Higher power.

Indeed, I was fast becoming conscious of the fact that I was merely a beneficiary of this great light of knowledge — not necessarily its creator. Moreover, it did not mean that I became instantly 'all knowing' and knew and understood everything that there was to know about everything, as the type of knowledge that I could access was strictly limited. It was dependent on my current level of knowledge and understanding. Just as a child in kindergarten would not have the ability to grasp the rudiments of calculus or advanced mathematics, there has to be a certain level of *mental* development before knowledge can build upon itself.

In other words, I would still remain an ignoramus in those fields of knowledge where I had not taken the time or trouble to develop my mind, even amidst this great and shining light of knowledge. More than anything else, I saw that it required an introspective or thinking person to appreciate the deeper truths of the higher realms. Thus, developing our intellects and widening our knowledge base while on Earth definitely paved the way for us to tap into this vast reservoir of light and knowledge of the sixth dimension.

For some inscrutable reason, I found myself gravitating towards matters of philosophy and deep theosophical thought, in spite of the fact that I had not formally pursued either during my present lifetime. As I marveled at my new-found thirst for such knowledge, I caught a fleeting flashback of myself as a young student of philosophy standing on the steps of a Parthenon-like structure in ancient Greece. This suggested to me a strong link between past-life conditioning and my present inclination towards matters of philosophy. It also drove home to me the fact that acquiring knowledge was an ever-evolving and cumulative process that spanned *several* lifetimes, and far beyond the scope of a single lifetime.

I could now understand how there are no child prodigies or instant geniuses born into the world. They are essentially wise old souls packaged into brand new bodies who drew their inspiration and creative genius from the mind-expanding light of the sixth dimension. Moreover, I discovered that the mind of a so-called 'genius' is really a window into the Infinite mind of God and a gift to the world. Like the renaissance men of old, they too are individuals who have dared to dream and reach *beyond* themselves to bring forth a great flowering of knowledge and creative wisdom into the world.

The acid test for all true knowledge, however, is how well one is able to transform knowledge from its more abstract and numinous state into a practical and usable form for the benefit of humanity. Bringing back a vacant or abstract memory from this plane of mental inspiration in and of itself is not enough. In order for creative vision and inspired thought to be of use, it needs to be *worked upon* and made accessible to the people in a pragmatic way. Thomas Edison, inventor of the light bulb who applied the principles of mass production to the process of invention, certainly knew what he was talking about when he coined the phrase, *"Genius is one percent inspiration, ninety-nine percent perspiration."*

In other words, what matters is how well we can harness and utilize our special knowledge, intellect or God-given talent, for the good of all mankind. Ultimately, what counts is *how well we have managed to serve our fellow man.* But it is not just a matter of recognizing the essential brotherhood of man as an abstract or ideological concept. It is actively applying and *demonstrating* that principle in real life in the true spirit of charity and brotherhood. Therefore, in order to make it into the sixth dimension, we truly need to act as ONE people. It means putting aside our differences and to start thinking in terms of a common body of humanity working together in the interest of the common good.

* * *

Every dimension, I discovered, has a certain type of thinking that dominates its consciousness. While the primary focus on the lower dimensions is on improving *ourselves*, the focus on the higher dimensions shifts dramatically from self-improvement to improvement of the masses and humanity as a whole. Its thinking moves beyond the exclusive development of a *personal* conscience and revolves around cultivating a *social* conscience. This means bringing the fundamental premise of personal ethics to bear on the fast-advancing fields of science, technology and other areas of human endeavor. It means studying the *real* impact of a particular scientific or knowledge-based discovery upon the human element in society. And it means safeguarding the interests of a larger sector of community, as opposed to looking solely to our own needs and individual self-interests.

Developing a social conscience requires that we not only enlarge the scope of our thinking, but we become less insular and more inclusive in our outlook. It means taking broader social issues such as climate change, global warming, environmental pollution, wildlife preservation, world peace, world hunger, global poverty, child mortality, bio-ethics and other pertinent 21st century issues and treating them like our own. Above all, it means cultivating a sense of *unity consciousness* amongst all peoples and coming together as one *in spirit* at least during our lifetimes on earth. In short, it means striving to make a difference in the world around us, as opposed to only within ourselves.

The main emphasis on the higher realms of consciousness, therefore, is cultivating a spirit of generosity, of caring
and sharing that goes *beyond* the needs of the individual 'self.'
Indeed, one way of forgetting ourselves and acquiring the
necessary humility in the process is to focus on the needs of
others. I found that the most effective way of doing this is
through the act of service. That is, to voluntarily seek to serve
our fellow man regardless of race, color, class, religion, creed
or political persuasion.

Service, of course, takes different forms. It involves the
voluntary sharing of our time, knowledge, wealth or means.
But whatever form it takes, service is often undertaken out of
a sense of moral obligation, or a way of paying one's dues to
society. At other times it is rendered out of a genuine sense
of compassion and concern for others, as well as a means of
alleviating suffering in the world. But whether the service is
obligatory, philanthropic, altruistic, humanitarian or simply
devotional, it needs to be performed without remuneration
or expectation of material gain. Above all, it requires an
unwavering commitment and devotion to a cause greater
than ourselves.

True service, therefore, is never selfish or self-serving. It is
something that is given freely and undertaken solely for the
sake of service. In fact, service, I discovered, is really an *active*
form of love, where any act of genuine human kindness is
considered '*love in action*.' Service then becomes the ultimate
form of prayer, where a single good deed is often worth a
thousand prayers. It is infinitely more effective than prayer
that is performed mindlessly, without emotion or thought.

In order to be able to go beyond even the sixth dimension, it was firmly impressed upon my mind that we needed to first go that extra mile *in life*. This did not mean paying lip service, but actively *demonstrating* that love and generosity of spirit to those less fortunate amongst us. Thus, one of the most profound realizations I made was that *any* act of service performed with a genuine and heartfelt desire to serve, is considered to be the highest form of worship. For, to serve man or God's many creations is to serve God. It, indeed, validates our reason for being and very existence on Earth.

Therefore, service without a doubt remains the quickest and surest way of getting closer to God. In the end, it is only through the process of forgetting ourselves, and merging our sense of self-identity with the greater good of the cause that we are serving, that we can truly hope to lose ourselves in the *essence* that is God.

* * *

Pure unconditional love — or plain devotion, often forms the basis of all true service. In fact, *love*, I discovered, is the highest emotion there is, and is the *only* emotion capable of transporting us beyond the sixth dimension of mystical and inspired thought.

Even as I made this realization, I found myself yearning for the real and more tangible presence of my Beloved Lord. The next thing I knew, I was being withdrawn from the mind-expanding spotlight and found myself emerge somewhere high above the open-air coliseum. I once again found myself suspended in the dusky twilight of yet another veil.

I again saw myself as a well-defined body of light contained within the gentle confines of my 'golden' suit. The full relevance of this shiny one-piece garment now became clear to me. It had acted as a protective armor, shielding me from the all-consuming power of the spotlight, while at the same time allowing me to experience the full intensity and illumination of my own light. Consequently, I managed to emerge unscathed, fully cognizant of who I was and where exactly it was that I was headed.

As I tried to gather my bearings, I could see the faraway glow of a solitary light closing in on me from my right. And before I knew it, standing there beside me in all His shining glory was the dazzling and incandescent figure of my Beloved Lord. The deep longing and affection in my heart had procured His overwhelming presence before me. What seemed odd, however, was the fact that He appeared to be in *two* places at the same time — both by my side, and at the zenith and farthest point of my horizon.

The next thing I knew, I was being totally consumed by the galvanizing touch of His right hand upon on my left shoulder. Like a dazed moth ready to self-destruct and annihilate itself off the face of all creation, I found myself being irresistibly and magnetically drawn into His Light. But as I zeroed in on His Light, it seemed to give way to an even greater Light as I approached the zenith and farthest point of my horizon. Even as I relinquished my hold on that insignificant little flicker of consciousness that was 'me,' I found myself being engulfed by wave upon wave of infinite Light.

It was like being swept into a great big Ocean of Light. I felt like a tiny leaf being tossed about in a tempestuous sea. As I surrendered myself to the Ocean, I found myself being imperceptibly drawn into the deeper and calmer waters beneath, where everything was incredibly still. Even as I melded into the stillness, I realized that my lone leaf no longer existed separate and apart from the almighty Ocean. 'I,' or that part that used to be me, became the Light and the Light became 'me.' I had bridged that final gap of separation and crossed over into the seventh dimension.

* * *

Everything else that followed seemed surreal as I blurred into a singularly sublime state of nothingness, or more precisely, an *everythingness* that cannot be described. The tiny pinpoint of my consciousness had somehow merged into the all-encompassing consciousness of an infinite Universe. I felt a sense of complete and absolute interconnectedness to *all* levels of life — both animate and inanimate, as well as everything in between.

I was no longer conscious of myself existing as a separate individual or entity of light, but seemed to embrace a kind of all-enveloping consciousness that did not differentiate between man or beast, vegetable or mineral, form or non-form. I was outside time and space. I was both the sun and the moon. I was the wind, the water, as well as the desert storm. In fact, I *was* the Universe — from the loftiest moun-taintop to the tiniest speck of dust on the ground. But rather than being the actual particle of matter that made up the Universe, I saw myself as a pale rose-colored energy that flowed *between the spaces* in the particles of matter that made up the vegetable, mineral, or rock.

It was seeing eternity in a grain of sand. It was *being* the delicate blush of a rose, as well as the steadfastness of a rock, the exquisite grace and beauty of a free-spirited horse, and the rounded perfection of a dewdrop. It was being both the leaves as well as the breeze that reverberated amongst the leaves, and it was being the 'sap' within the sap of a tree.

It was as though the Universe and everything in it was a giant sponge that was immersed in this great big Ocean of Light, where not only was everything in the Ocean but the Ocean was in everything too. In other words, not only are we a part of God's Light, but it is also a part of us. It is directly experiencing God and the truth behind those immortal words: *"Everything lives, moves and has its being in God."*

At the level of the Absolute, when all veils and mists of illusion have finally been lifted, God is the *only* reality that exists. The distinction between the message and the messenger disappears, the raindrop becomes the river, and the river becomes the Almighty Ocean. Everything is every-thing and ALL, indeed, becomes ONE.

* * *

Experiencing this truth was the finest hour of my existence. It was my shining moment of truth, as well as the culmination of all my lives lived on Earth. It was that single blessed moment of becoming for which I had lived and struggled through all my lives. Even as I reached the full climax of my experience, I felt 'myself' spontaneously separate from this great vortex of Light and inner calm.

I could feel myself being shunted to the outer edge and periphery of my existence by a centrifugal force that I felt powerless to resist. As I spiraled rapidly downwards and out of the Light, I could hardly contain the sense of absolute joy and elation that pervaded my being. I felt like a whirling dervish descending back from an alternate reality as I pirouetted ecstatically around the shores of my fourth-dimensional landscape in a state of drunken euphoria.

For some strange reason, I found myself embodied in the consciousness of a playful and frolicking little dolphin. It was like going from the supremely sublime to the downright ridiculous. Even as I marveled at the sheer absurdity of my situation, I found myself communicating with two older, more sedate looking dolphins. They were urging me to plunge back into the waters of my physical world as time had once again become of the essence.

I hesitated briefly as I did not yet want to relinquish my hold on this newfound world of joy, happiness and boundless freedom. But I was swiftly reminded of my 'mission' and the commitment I had made to return. As I prepared to make my final descent back into the physical world, I noticed a large gray whale lingering close to the shoreline. Its serious demeanor and sheer lack of joy seemed to have a strangely dampening effect on my spirit. I felt myself shiver as I watched the faint glimmering of pinkish light caress the early morning sky. As I dove reluctantly into the frigid waters, the lights dimmed out and everything palled into insignificance.

CHAPTER SEVEN

Baptism by Fire

I had to keep reminding myself that just as the purity of a precious metal is tested in fire, so is the human spirit tested in the fire of suffering. And like that immortal and legendary phoenix, I would once again rise from the fire and ashes of my own destruction ...

*A*s I came crashing down to earth, I had a distinct sense of being guided back into my present reality by a supersonic vibration imperceptible to the human ear. And it was a bit of an anticlimax to once again find myself hovering over my still and lifeless body at the Celebration Hospital in Orlando.

I could see several doctors and members of the medical staff working on me from above. But my attention seemed to be riveted on one of the doctors standing at my bedside. He appeared strangely vivified and surrounded by a bluish white light. He had apparently uttered a silent prayer prior to commencing some procedure on me, and seemed quite unaware of the divine power he had commanded to his side by that single gesture of faith. His aura somehow appeared brighter than anyone else in the room and I found myself being involuntarily drawn towards that light.

It looked like his prayers were answered as I found myself fuse into what felt like a carcass of meat. I felt like ice. Even though they had succeeded in reviving me and resuscitating me back to life, I was hanging onto life by a thread. My left lung had collapsed, my kidneys had failed and my blood pressure was dangerously low. My pulse was weak and my heart rate erratic. Apart from the existing complications of the pancreatitis, I had developed pneumonia, had fluid in my lungs, and was in congestive heart failure. All the major organs in my body were beginning to shut down and seize due to infection, or sepsis.

According to the hospital records I had stopped breathing and gone into respiratory failure on December 22nd, 1998 between the early morning hours of 4:05 and 4:25 a.m. By 4:30 a.m., the hospital had already contacted my husband Amin, requesting that he come over despite the dense fog and poor visibility outside. By the time he arrived at the hospital with our two boys, he was stunned to find me in a coma, on life support and in a state of total paralysis. The last thing that he had expected was to see me on my deathbed, suspended as I was between life and death.

Two of the attending physicians had taken Amin aside and briefed him on the seriousness of my condition. They informed him that they had done everything that was medically possible and in their power to do, and suggested that the only thing anyone could do for me now was to pray and call in a pastor.

As he leafed through the Orlando phone directory in a state of complete shock and disbelief, he realized that finding a pastor from our particular denomination at that time of the morning, in a strange and unfamiliar land, was not going to be easy. But after making a few inquiries through Calgary, he was finally able to contact a distant relation who had moved to Orlando from Calgary a few years back. And within the hour, I had not one but two ministers by my side administering me my last rites (*Madhan Chaanto*) in accordance with the Shia Ismaili Muslim tradition of my faith.

My condition at that point was considered far too grave to have me physically moved to an operating room to undergo a critical cardiac catheterization procedure that could help determine the cause of my respiratory and multiple organ failure. However, in the wake of a decision to perform the procedure inside my hospital room, a faint glimmer of hope began to surface as the doctors managed to regulate my heartbeat and re-inflate my lung. My blood pressure was up again, and my kidneys were beginning to function normally.

Although they had managed to stabilize me, I was not quite out of the woods yet. Along with the complications of the pneumonia and the raging infection, there was a significant worsening of my pancreatitis. I remained anemic despite receiving several transfusions of blood, and continued to have dangerously low levels of blood calcium which, in turn, was preventing the antibiotics from taking effect.

121

In addition to the high fever and infection, there was also the more immediate threat of clot formation at the site of my central line. Thus, my prognosis was never good. I remained in critical condition as each day continued to pose a fresh challenge. My chances of survival or actually making it, remained at around ten percent. My husband was even asked to notify the family and prepare them for the worst.

But through it all, one thing remained abundantly clear. It was the overwhelming show of support that we received from members of the Ismaili community in Orlando. Even though they did not know us personally, they had rallied around and organized support groups for Amin and the boys, as well as other members of my family that were beginning to arrive from Calgary. They had whole-heartedly opened their hearts and homes to us, providing round-the-clock support as they stood vigil by my bedside and held special prayers for my recovery.

Their actions clearly spoke louder than their words, and it is something that we will always remain eternally grateful for. In reaching out to us as they did, not only did they demon-strate the true meaning of compassion and selfless service, but they strengthened and re-affirmed the bonds of frontier-less brotherhood that have existed in the Ismaili community for nearly fourteen hundred years of our history.

There was also no shortage of well-wishers from members of the wider community. The Christian nurses and staff at the hospital, too, had lit many a candle for my recovery. A woman from New Jersey whose husband had suffered a heart attack while vacationing in Florida, had brought me a special 'angel pin' to watch over me in hospital. There was also the

Christmas tree that was given to us by a British family whose mother had passed away in the room next to mine. And there were the many get-well cards and baskets of fruit left at my bedside in a gesture of goodwill from total strangers who were never likely to see me again.

Even though I was not conscious of what was going on around me at the time, I know that this generous outpouring of support from the people of Orlando had meant the difference between hope and despair for my family. It gave them the courage and strength to endure that difficult time, knowing they were not alone. Above all, it helped rekindle our faith in human goodness and our innate capacity for genuine kindness towards our fellow wayfarers on Earth.

It was pretty much touch and go for me for the next few days that followed, but the fact remained that I was still alive. And so long as I was alive, there was hope. As family, friends and even total strangers continued to pray for my recovery, I kept beating the odds and my condition gradually started to improve. However, despite several attempts to extubate me, I still remained on a respirator unable to breathe on my own.

* * *

The ten or eleven days that I spent in hospital in Orlando seemed to blend into each other as I remained in a medically induced coma and semi-conscious for the most part. Even incidents which would normally have left their mark on me were completely erased from my memory. Memory loss or amnesia, as I later found out, was one of the common side effects of sedation and the medication being administered to manage my pain.

But amidst the amnesia, I still seemed to recall a few lucid moments of conscious recollection that felt more real to me than anything I could possibly have dreamt. My first moment of such awareness since coming back from the brink of death came, of all days, on Christmas Day. I remember feeling extremely weak, cold and disorientated. My body felt as heavy as lead and I literally felt like death warmed over, as I found myself being aroused from a deep, drug-induced sleep. I could hear an incessant buzzing noise in my ear, like the sound of a pesky little fly trapped in my head.

As I became more coherent, it slowly registered upon my mind somewhere that it was a message of Christmas greeting being conveyed to me in a very broad Swahili accent — just the way I remembered it back in my days of growing up in Kenya! As it turned out, my sister Shainaz had spoken to the boys from Calgary and coached them to relay the greeting to me in that particular fashion. After its initial impact however, it began to feel increasingly like a stuck recording that was starting to wear extremely thin on my nerves.

I later discovered that extreme irritability, disorientation, and agitation to the point of aggression were apparently quite common in persons coming out of a coma — and I certainly was no exception. However, the good news was that I was exhibiting some sign of normal brain activity and was at least neurologically intact. And so it was hardly surprising that in my next moment of conscious recollection, I found my arms and hands securely strapped to the bed!

For some reason I remember being more aware of what was going on *outside* my room, rather than inside. It almost felt like a dream where I thought I had clearly seen my two boys standing outside my hospital room in their white T-shirts, along with a friend from Calgary in blue shirt sleeves whom I had known since the 1970s. From what I could make out, they were straining to see inside the half-shuttered window of my hospital room in Intensive Care. I thought it a little odd at the time and had even wondered why they did not come into the room like everyone else.

I later found out that I had not been dreaming. Apparently, that friend from Calgary in the blue shirt had also been vacationing in Florida at the time and had generously offered to take the boys out for the day. I also found out that my sons had been strictly forbidden to enter my room, as every time they came in I would get extremely excited and agitated, setting off all the alarms on the various monitors that I was hooked up to.

In another memory flash, I could have sworn that I had heard the reassuring sound of my mother's voice penetrate the wavering thread of my consciousness. I could feel her comforting presence by my side — amidst the nausea and feverish deliriums, and the cylindrical device that suctioned out a vile-looking liquid from my stomach. As I later learned, I had not been hearing voices as my mother had, indeed, flown in from Calgary and had been constantly at my bedside in hospital.

* * *

After spending a total of eleven days in Intensive Care at the Celebration Health Hospital in Orlando, I was finally deemed stable enough to be airlifted back to Canada. I was transported via air ambulance, under heavy sedation and close medical supervision, to the Peter Lougheed Hospital in Calgary, Alberta on December 30th, 1998.

Although I have no conscious recollection of the trip back, or the day that followed, January 1st, 1999, however, stands out quite vividly in my mind. I recall being aroused from a heavy, drugged-induced sleep by the familiar voices of my husband and sister, who informed me that I was back in Calgary and that it was New Year's Day. That date for some reason seemed to ring a bell somewhere at the back of my mind, and I remember being overcome with emotion as I realized that it was also Amin's birthday!

Being able to dredge up a clear memory of his birth date from within the fuzzy layers of my consciousness was in itself a personal breakthrough for me. It meant that I was once again able to reconnect with my physical environment in a *conscious* sort of way. I was now on home turf, with family and friends, amidst familiar surroundings. Life no longer resembled one drawn-out moment of drugged existence, but suddenly seemed infused with periods of increased recollection, meaning, and even hope.

By January 4th, the pancreatitis was beginning to subside without any trace of abscess formation and I was finally extubated and weaned off the ventilator. But it was a short-lived victory as, only two days later, around 4:50 a.m. I had to once again be re-intubated due to acute respiratory distress and obstruction of my airways. I was exhibiting the classic signs of superior vena cava syndrome, and had developed extensive clots in my great vessels at the site of the central line due to infection, or sepsis. My subclavian and internal jugular veins were completely blocked, causing congestion and swelling in my face, neck, chest and upper extremities.

For the next few days that followed I remained heavily sedated in Intensive Care, totally oblivious of what was going on in the world around me. Everything once again began to blur as I drifted in and out of consciousness. When I finally regained consciousness, I wondered why everyone was making such a fuss over me. Surrounded as I was by the many monitors, equipment and machinery, I was beginning to feel overwhelmingly like a demented pincushion that had its stuffing knocked out of it. I realized then, that my road to recovery was going to be a slow and painful one, and one that I would essentially have to walk alone.

Although I was kept in strict isolation for the next several days, I seemed generally more cognizant of my surroundings and the people that interspersed my space. But with this awareness also came the stinging realization of my pain and intense physical discomfort, which now seemed all too real. My only respite came from sleep and the morphine that not only helped numb my pain, but also served to thoroughly disorientate me. The worst part of it was the hallucinations and total lack of connection with reality that occurred upon first being aroused from a morphine-induced stupor. Then, of course, there was also the dreaded late night and early morning suctioning of my lungs.

Yet, amidst it all, I had no clue whatsoever of my close brush with death. Apart from those brief memory flashes that were later confirmed to be true, I had no real recollection of my stay in hospital in Florida. As a result, I had no inkling of the traumatic turn of events that had transpired in my life — except for the fact that I was living through my own private hell. And from what little I could gather, I knew there was nothing I could do but pray and just hope for the best.

As I continued to waft in and out of consciousness, the dominant thoughts in my waking moments of consciousness seemed to somehow center around water, or more precisely the lack of it. Of all the things that I had to endure, the hardest to bear was the burning sensation of thirst in my throat. Between the high fevers, the effect of the antibiotics, the anticoagulants, and the aggressive diuresis employed to reduce the swelling and pressure on my airways, I felt like I was in the desert and my throat perpetually on fire.

Apparently, the whole focus of my prescribed course of treatment had revolved around keeping me as dry as possible, to prevent fluid build-up inside my lungs and congestion in the vessels outside. This raging inferno inside my throat was, by far, the most agonizing aspect of my ordeal and the closest thing that resembled hell. It was not until many months later that I found out, due to the precarious state of my health and the risk of internal hemorrhage, to have done *anything* differently would have been to literally kill me.

It was only in hindsight that I realized with a sense of irony, that enduring the fire of my ferocious thirst *without* water — the very substance that sustained life, was what saved my life. In the meantime, I had to keep reminding myself that just as the purity of a precious metal is tested in fire, so is the human spirit tested in the fire of suffering. But as hard as I tried to be philosophical about it, the reality was that the truth sucked and I continued to protest vehemently against my forced deprivation of water.

Not yet fully aware of the fight to keep me alive, I continued to wallow in self-pity and suffer in silence *'the slings and arrows of my outrageous fortune.'* While thirst without a doubt topped my list of grievances in hospital, not being able to communicate with the outside world was just as frustrating. Being on a ventilator meant that I could not talk — something that I had always taken for granted.

Fortunately for me, some of the nurses at the hospital had encouraged me to express myself on paper. This not only helped me vent out my frustrations, but to a large extent helped preserve my sanity. Of course, one of the first things I remember jotting down on paper was a polite request for a glass of water or, alternatively, a tall glass of freshly-squeezed orange juice! Although my particular requests were never met, and all I ever got was a cotton swabful or two of water to moisten my parched and dehydrated lips, it felt good just to be able to interact with others on a mental level once again.

Somehow, through it all, I managed to hang in there one painfully slow and agonizing day at a time. And, slowly but surely, I finally began to show signs of resolution from the swelling and the blood clots in my veins. I even found myself looking forward to the day when I would feel that precious trickle of water going down my throat.

* * *

Thankfully, as all physical experiences that are of this earth are prone to do, my particular period of penance too came to an end. I was successfully extubated — without having to undergo a surgical tracheotomy, and was transferred out of Intensive Care into the General Ward on January 19, 1999.

Although I had been scheduled for a tracheotomy the day before, the operating theatre had become unavailable due to some last-minute emergency. Consequently, I was forced to remain an extra day on the respirator in Intensive Care. As it turned out, my last day on the respirator also happened to coincide with the last day of *Ramadan* — the holy month of fasting for Muslims all over the world.

As I counted back to the total number of days that I had spent in Intensive Care, I remember entering the hospital in Orlando on December 20th, 1998 — which, coincidentally, also happened to be the *first* day of Ramadan. It struck me that by staying that extra day in Intensive Care, I had in fact been physically forced to observe the fast for the *full* duration of Ramadan — which, in my case, turned out to be exactly thirty days, not a day less or a day more.

Apart from being physically restrained from taking in food or water for those thirty days, I realized that I had also been physically silenced due to the inordinately long period of time that I had to spend on the respirator. And it crossed my mind that, in keeping with the *true* spirit of Ramadan — which is to also refrain from all unkind thoughts, words or deeds — I had been forcibly restrained from uttering a mean or uncharitable word to anyone during those thirty days!

Traditionally associated with a time of self-discipline and physical housekeeping, and a time of increased spiritual reflection, I can only hope that I emerged from my particular period of fasting and penance a spiritually more aware person for it. Being compelled to observe the silence made me turn increasingly inwards, towards prayer and quiet contemplation. This act of silent submission and reflection, in many ways, turned out to be the most uplifting part of my stay in Intensive Care.

To finally be allowed to transfer out of Intensive Care was a liberating experience, and a reason in itself to celebrate. It was also the day of *Idd-ul-Fitr* — a day of great festivity and celebration that marked the official end of Ramadan. Even though I still remained tethered to my intravenous pole, I felt ridiculously free. I could not quite believe that I was no longer bound to the countless equipment and machinery that had been my steady companions for the past thirty days. And like that immortal and legendary phoenix, I could once again feel myself rise from the fire and ashes of my own destruction.

CHAPTER EIGHT

A Reason to Celebrate

Transferring out of Intensive Care was a reason in itself for me to celebrate. It felt good to be alive and breathing on my own. It was also the day of Idd-ul-Fitr, a day of great festivity and celebration that marked the official end of Ramadan ...

*T*he day of *Idd-ul-Fitr* itself turned out to be a day of great rejoicing and personal celebration that promised of better things to come. As I found myself being wheeled into the General Ward directly opposite the nurses' station, I realized with a sense of quiet elation that I was once again back in the land of the living. It felt good to be alive and to be able to breathe on my own without the help of a ventilator. What was absolutely the highlight of my day, however, was a quarter cup of the most delicious and succulent chips of ice to ever grace my parched and dehydrated lips.

After about a month on a ventilator and a feeding tube, the gnawing pangs of hunger had completely subsided and I had no appetite to speak of. My thirst, however, seemed to have intensified with each passing day. Thus, breaking my month-long fast and celebrating my release from Intensive Care with a handful of ice-chips seemed to be the most appropriate way to end my fast. It was also one of the most deeply satisfying and life-affirming experiences of my life.

As I sat there contently sucking on my little stockpile of ice, I appreciated how good it felt to be alive and actually breathing on my own. As I settled into my new environment in the General Ward, I noticed how everything appeared so much brighter and livelier than in Intensive Care. However, things changed quite drastically in the next few hours as I recall being aroused from a vague and uneasy sleep around midnight, with a nauseous feeling in the pit of my stomach. The last thing I remember as I reached for the buzzer was keeling over the rails on the side of my bed.

Despite the fact that the nurses' station was located only a few yards across the hall from my room, it was a full twenty minutes before I found myself being hoisted back into position by a kindly-looking night nurse. As I stared at the puddle of bile-colored liquid that I had spewed out on the floor several minutes before, it struck me that things worked a little differently here on the General Ward.

For a start, the patient to nurse ratio was considerably higher here than the one-on-one attention that I was accustomed to in Intensive Care. Also, there seemed to be less of a sense of urgency here, and everything seemed much more laid back in general. They appeared to march to the beat of a different drummer here, unlike in Intensive Care where they routinely faced potentially life-threatening situations every minute of the day.

I soon learned that I had been completely weaned off the morphine and, as a result, was experiencing the usual symptoms of morphine withdrawal. So for the next several days that followed, I was not quite as bright-eyed and bushy-tailed as I had been upon my arrival into the General Ward. Although the chills, the jitters, the nausea and the intolerable night sweats finally did subside, my thirst still remained largely unabated.

The bland diet of thickened liquids and pureed mush did little to allay the fire and misery of my thirst. Due to the long length of time that I had been on the respirator, I remained at high risk for asphyxiation due to fluid travelling down to my lungs. My voice remained hoarse and barely audible, but the good news was that I had not suffered permanent damage to my vocal cords and things could only improve with time.

It was not until nine or ten days later that I was finally allowed some clear liquid into my system. After a few false starts and what seemed like an eternity, my prayers were finally answered. I remember the great pains that Terry, my speech therapist at the hospital, had taken to ensure that my first sip would be my beverage of choice as she scoured the hospital floors in search of my favorite drink. Fortunately for me, she did not come back empty-handed.

It was a day that I had eagerly awaited and played over in my mind many times. I had literally lived for the day that I could feel the refreshing tickle of an ice-cold ginger ale swishing around in my throat. So after a long and grueling period of almost six weeks without any fluids, the day finally arrived for me to take in my first sip of exquisite bliss. I was not disappointed. It was pure heaven, everything I had imagined and more. And by the time I managed to down a full glass of the golden liquid, I had extinguished most of the fire that had raged uncontrollably inside me for the past forty days.

After a few days of monitored dosage my thirst finally subsided, and I began to feel increasingly more at peace with myself. I felt a deep sense of calm and release and an over-whelming sense of gratitude for God's many bounties in my life. I vowed never to take any of the blessings in my life — especially water, for granted again. In surviving this long spell of drought in my life, I felt I must surely have atoned in some small measure at least, for whatever karmic infraction that I may have carried over from my past — as there is *always* a point to our suffering. I just hoped that mine had not been in vain.

* * *

In the days that followed, everything seemed rosier and brighter and I began to feel generally more optimistic about life again. Even the twice-a-day bane of being poked and prodded by what I fondly referred to as those 'blood-sucking vampires' who came in for their daily sampling of blood, seemed tolerable now. The humiliation and indignity of enduring those dreadful little sponge baths and lopsided bedpans, too, was more bearable. And so after surviving that initial period without water or the morphine, I found myself slowly croaking back into existence and the more humanized environment of the General Ward.

One of the more memorable things about being in the General Ward was that I was no longer muzzled up or on a respirator. In other words, I could now *talk!* I could engage in the pleasurable art of verbal communication and carry on a serious two-way conversation with someone other than myself. Whether or not anyone understood what I had to say was, of course, another matter entirely. Just the fact that I could interact somewhat normally with family, friends and members of the medical staff, made me once again feel like a part of the human race. Their interest in me now seemed more personal, as opposed to wholly clinical, and I no longer felt like a science experiment or someone who had just had her wings clipped.

One of my first two-way exchanges in hospital occurred with a wonderful woman by the name of Marla. She was the first daytime nurse assigned to me on the General Ward. Her no-nonsense manner, ready wit and cheerful air of optimism endeared her to me immediately. She would come into my room every morning and take a moment to take in the view of the majestic Rockies that was visible from my window on a clear day. Even on days that I was not on her normal roster of patients, I looked forward to her little visits when she would come in and share her joke of the day, or simply gaze outside the window and admire the view.

Of course, there were other nurses who were equally as kind and gracious whose names I cannot remember, but whose faces are permanently etched on my mind. There were also other members of the medical staff who were just as caring, including a couple of young doctors on the ward, as well as the orderlies who brought in my meals, my physical and speech therapists, and the dietician who monitored my meals. Whether it was their kind words of encouragement, their small gestures of generosity, or just their friendly smiles, they managed to brighten my day and make a difference in ways that they will never know.

My long stay in hospital made me realize that nursing is truly one of the most honorable professions that exists. It is a high and noble calling which, ironically, is also one that is often the most under-appreciated. It was only in being directly at the receiving end of their kindness that I came to recognize their true worth. I saw them as my little angels of mercy who watched over me whilst I slept, or stayed awake at night, and helped me make sense of my world that had been so abruptly turned upside down.

So whether it was nurses like Lila and Carol in Florida, or Marla, Shauna, Terry and Robyn in Calgary, it was people like them that made my life a little more tolerable in hospital. It made me realize that nurses are a blessing to humanity. They deserve our highest respect and gratitude for the many thankless tasks that they perform to alleviate suffering in the world.

With the blessing of water and human interaction back in my life again, I was able to think more clearly. I realized that not only was I lucky to be alive, but I had a lot to be thankful for in my life. As I looked around, my heart filled with joy and gratitude at the symbols of love and great outpouring of support that surrounded me. The sight of the many flowers and cards from well-wishers, family, friends and even total strangers, was both gratifying and at the same time humbling.

Compared to my dim and austere surroundings in Intensive Care, the General Ward was positively brimming with life, color, laughter and joy. As I slowly began to appreciate that my life from this point onwards was a gift, I recognized however that the greater gift in my life was the gift of love and friendship and being amongst people who cared.

* * *

Water for some reason seemed to play a vital and pivotal role in my healing process. I can vividly recall the day when my daytime nurse Marla, that pragmatic soul of compassion, asked me if I was up to having a shower. By now all the morphine had more or less cleared out of my system, and I was beginning to feel dull and jaded and thoroughly worn out from the whole ordeal. So after more than a month of messy and wholly inadequate sponge baths, those blessed words were like music to my wax-plugged ears!

Between juggling with the soap, manipulating the chrome levers, and holding down the plastic bags taped to my intravenous lines, I felt that I had perhaps bitten-off more than I could chew. But as I got better coordinated and allowed the soothing properties of the water to run over me, I could feel the inner tension and intense physical weariness begin to melt and drain right out with the bath water.

Incredibly, taking that long and refreshing shower turned out to be more than a physical experience. It felt like a deeply spiritual experience, the kind that touches your soul. And as I emerged out of the shower feeling thoroughly revitalized from the inside out, I could not help jokingly remark to Marla that it felt like I had just died and gone to heaven!

The moment I uttered those seemingly innocuous words, I could feel the heavy yoke of burden lift from my shoulders. As I embraced that overwhelming sense of freedom, it felt like something inside me had changed. It was as though the very act of immersing myself in water had sparked-off a chain reaction within the deepest layers of my consciousness, and opened wide the floodgates of memory. And, bit by bit, the dense fog of my amnesia began to lift. As the mists of forgetfulness started to clear from my head, fascinating little details from my so-called 'experience' began to rapidly fill my mind.

For some reason the images that filtered through my head seemed to come in reverse order. Intermittently at first, and then more quickly, the images began to gush spontaneously forth onto the unsuspecting mantle of my mind. Starting with the moment I saw myself merge with the Light of my Lord, to fusing joyously with the consciousness of a dolphin, I started to regress all the way back to the moment I first saw my Dad, before finally finding myself suspended on the ceiling over my hospital bed in Florida.

It gradually sank in that something quite dramatic and life changing had happened to me — somewhere between arriving in Florida and returning to Calgary — that had shunted me directly into the orbit of another world. As I started to press my family for more detail, it became increasingly clear that I had somehow crossed over into an alternate reality that was unlike any other I had known.

Up until now, I did not have a clue as to my close call with death, since it was not exactly the type of information that one would voluntarily share with someone in a semi-conscious state. But now that the memory of my contact with a white Light, as well as coming face to face with a younger, more vibrant version of my Dad had managed to surface, my curiosity was definitely piqued.

As I slowly started to gather fascinating little tidbits of information from my stay in Florida, it struck me that God certainly had a delicious sense of irony. Paradoxically, it was precisely during the early morning hours of December 22nd, 1998 — the day of the Winter solstice that year, and what is generally considered to be the darkest day of the year — that He chose to reveal to me the full splendor and glory of His Light.

* * *

Having a vivid recollection of an alternate reality that is dramatically different from your present reality, has a way of changing your perspective on life — and one that raises a million questions in your mind. But because the memory of the experience had come so thick and fast and erupted so suddenly onto my mind, the information was far too over-whelming for me to process at once. Even though I knew deep down in my heart that I had crossed that thin line which separates life from death, it was not something that I was quite ready to shout out from the rooftops.

I, nevertheless, must have inadvertently let that odd remark slip here and there as, before long, I had several visitors and well-wishers filing into my room openly curious about my 'experience' with the Light. Although their interest in me was genuine, and nobody seemed to ridicule me, the fear of being thought of as 'crazy' prevented me from revealing too much. What seemed strange was the fact that they actually believed in what little I had to say. In fact, I have to admit that they were far more accepting of it than I might perhaps have been had our roles been reversed.

It wasn't that I did not believe in my own experience, but it had more to do with my own feelings of self-worth. It was a matter of my feeling spiritually inadequate of having merited the grace of such an incredible experience in my life. I could not help wonder how someone like me had come to experience such true and profound treasures of that other world, in what seemed like the blink of an eye. So until such time as I was *consciously* able to recognize my own worth and fully embrace my truth, I felt it best to keep my mouth shut.

Before I could bring myself to openly share my experience, I felt I needed to first independently assess the validity of my experience *in my own mind*. As I lay awake at night, privately mulling over in my mind things that I dared not talk about, I seemed to recall purchasing a book by Betty Eadie, just the day before I landed in hospital in Florida. From what I could recollect, she had documented her near-death experience in the book — something, I felt, could help me put my own experience into clearer perspective.

141

As I leafed through the book that Amin had managed to retrieve from my still unpacked suitcase, one of the first things that jumped out at me and caught my attention was a passage in the 'Foreword' written by Melvin Melrose, M.D. He wrote: *"Near-death experiences are not caused by a lack of oxygen to the brain or drugs, or psychological stresses evoked by the fear of dying. Almost twenty years of scientific research has documented that these experiences are a natural and normal process. We have even documented an area in the brain, which allows us to have the experience. That means near-death experiences are absolutely real and not hallucinations of the mind."*

Stumbling upon this fascinating piece of information that came from a medical doctor and *bona fide* member of the scientific community no less, blew me away. It certainly made me sit up and take notice. It independently confirmed to me that what I had experienced was *not* necessarily a hallucination, and forced me to re-evaluate my experience in a whole new light. I could no longer dismiss it as just another 'dream' or something that was too far-fetched to be 'real.'

In spite of our very diverse religious and cultural backgrounds, Ms. Eadie's compelling account of her journey into the spirit world helped me acknowledge my own near-death experience. Although there was a gap of over twenty-five years between our respective experiences, there were apparently some things in heaven that did not change. At the same time, I recognized that it was ultimately the state of our individual consciousness *in life* that would determine our particular experiences at death.

The notions of 'heaven' and 'hell' for me have always been temporary states of mind. What I had been searching for all my life was something more real and more substantive — such as the state of being that I had briefly experienced in the Light. Moreover, as I personally never had any doubt in my mind as to God's existence, and the fact that our spirit survived physical death, I did not seem to have the need for external proof of God's person in order to believe in His existence. Although belief in an *unseen* God is the ultimate test of one's faith — especially in a world driven by reason, science and logic, experiencing the *essence* that is God was, for me, the icing on the cake of my personal truth.

* * *

Although I have never thought of myself as an outwardly religious person, I have always had a deep and abiding faith in God and believe in the fundamental truth of all religions. Despite our varied rituals and linguistic differences, I knew in my heart that we all prayed to one and the *same* God. Thus, I have always held the firm conviction that anyone who lived by right and believed in God — or some Higher Intelligence, had equal access to His kingdom regardless of what religion he or she followed. To profess anything less would have been inconceivable to me.

Consequently, when I casually mentioned to my speech therapist, a practicing Christian, that I had experienced the actual moment of my death, I was totally unprepared for the reaction I got. I was surprised at the look of fear and pure panic that crossed her face. And with a hand that shook, she had reached for my hand and urgently pleaded for me to tell her that I believed in Jesus Christ!

Even though it seemed like an unusual thing to say to a Shiite Muslim such as myself, I assured her that not only did I categorically believe in Jesus Christ as being one of the divine apostles and Prophets of God, but so did *every* true Muslim around the world. In fact, to deny Jesus' stature as a prophet of God, or for that matter to deny any of God's accredited messengers — including Abraham, Moses, Noah, Muhammad, as well as the Virgin Mary herself, would be tantamount to denying Islam itself. An unmitigated belief in *all* of God's approximately 124,000 messengers, including His last prophet — the Prophet Muhammad, was central to the very doctrine of Islam.

Although she seemed a little taken aback by my answer, she was nevertheless very relieved to hear me openly profess my belief in Jesus Christ. She confessed that she had always been led to believe as a child that *only* Christians, or those who implicitly believed in Jesus Christ as their Lord and Savior, would be allowed to enter heaven or the kingdom of God. So more than anything else, she had been afraid that I might have been subjected to the fire and agonizing tortures that one traditionally associated with hell.

I suppose it is not uncommon to expect some elitist or misplaced notions of faith to exist, to some degree, in every religion in the world. Even though her words had seemed a little presumptuous, I realized that she actually meant well. As a matter of fact, as I recall, even Ms. Eadie had openly declared this same Christian view in her book. She wrote, she was told that, *"he [Jesus Christ] was the only door through which we will all return [and] he is the only door through which we can return."* Yet, judging from my own experiences on the other side, I knew that this was not always the case.

It made me realize that some statements are, indeed, born out of ignorance. It also helped open my eyes to the fact that I was perhaps a little more charitable and forgiving in my attitude towards other religions than they were towards mine. However, I bore no ill-will or animosity towards this wonderfully kind and caring individual who had tended so diligently to my vocal needs in hospital. At the same time, I did not feel it was quite my place to clear up any misconceptions she had in her mind about the other side, nor educate her on the legitimate place of *all* monotheistic faiths alike in the eternal kingdom of God.

Consequently, although I had grown quite fond of my speech therapist at the hospital, I could not bring myself to open up to her further. I also could not find it in my heart to 'shock and awe' her by telling her that despite being an avowed Muslim — and possibly a 'heathen' in her eyes, I had actually seen a vision of the Christ, along with one of the Virgin Mary, the Prophet Muhammad, and other accredited messengers of God. And so, even though I truly believed that Jesus *was* the way and a doorway to heaven for many, he was not the only way. In my experience, *all* roads led to Rome — or God.

* * *

I do not see myself as a religious activist or crusader of truth, but that single misconstrued statement about the ineligibility of non-Christians to enter heaven certainly gave me food for thought. It prompted me to take a closer look at my own experience and re-examine Ms. Eadie's Christian account of her near-death experience under a more analytical light.

Upon examining the essential elements in our respective experiences, I discovered that although there were indeed similarities, there were also some very obvious differences in our perspectives of life after death. Apart from those minor differences in the more physical aspects of our experiences, what stood out for me was that beyond the point of my 'life review,' I had also undergone an 'emotional clearing' and experienced the truth about reincarnation. Furthermore, the ability to visit several of my past lives and recognize some of the invaluable lessons I had learned from those lives, seemed to give credence to my own vague but pre-existing belief on the subject of reincarnation, personal accountability and karmic retribution.

Experiencing the great truth about reincarnation was for me like seeing the snow-capped peak of a mountain range on a *clear* day — something that is not always visible on a cloudy day. Similarly, it is only when the 'clouds of illusion' have been lifted from our minds that we are able to catch a glimpse of the truth — or the irrefutable reality that most definitely exists behind those clouds. But as the concept of reincarnation did not seem to form a part of Ms. Eadie's dominant beliefs in life, it was not something that she was likely to remember or experience in death. It is something that one has to personally grow into during the course of one's evolution.

Also, since I already had a pre-existing belief in the divine and exalted status of *all* of God's Prophets during my present lifetime, catching a glimpse of them was perhaps not all that unusual. What had intrigued me though, was encountering that strangely ovoid form of my 'emotional self' before coming face to face with the light of my own soul. It struck me that having an 'open mind' was definitely an asset in the spiritual realm — where the difference was not only a difference in degree, but a difference in *kind*.

Experiencing a state of consciousness that transcended the conventional notions of paradise, thought as well as form, made me wonder whether what I had experienced had perhaps bordered on the mystical. This element of mysticism, I realized, was actually quite commonplace in many eastern religions like my own — one that actively embraced the notion of a great formless mass of Intelligent Light and energy that permeated all levels of existence.

* * *

In the two or three weeks that I remained in the General Ward, I found that I had a lot of time on my hands to think and count the blessings in my life. Beyond what I had experienced on the other side, I felt extremely lucky to be alive and to be surrounded by people who cared, and I eagerly looked forward to the day that I could go home. As I got stronger, that day finally did arrive but under some rather strange and unusual circumstances.

Due to the broad spectrum of antibiotics and medications being administered intravenously, my tentative date of discharge was estimated to be sometime around the middle to end of February. But as fate would have it, one of the nurses had inadvertently stepped on the tubing connected to my central line, causing it to leak profusely. After several failed attempts to re-insert the line at various sites around my body — including my feet — the decision was finally made to convert the rest of my medication into pill or injectable form.

Of course, some of the pills that I ended up taking looked more like horse pills, large and cumbersome and difficult to swallow without gagging. But looking at it on the bright side, there now appeared to be a more than even chance that I would be discharged from hospital sooner rather than later, as intravenous therapy no longer seemed to be an option. This meant that I would not require the close monitoring and medical supervision I had needed earlier. Consequently, I anxiously awaited formal notification of my discharge from hospital.

I can recall that day clearly in my mind. It was February 4th, 1999, the day of Shafin's eleventh birthday. I remember thinking of him that day, wishing I could contact him at school and personally break the news to him. However, within minutes of thinking that, I received a surprise phone call from Shafin in hospital! Apparently, he had managed to memorize the last few digits on the telephone extension in my room the night before. He had been planning to surprise me with a phone call from school on his birthday — something that Mr. Roman, his wonderful Grade 6 teacher at the Prince of Wales Elementary School in Calgary, had kindly consented to. So when I asked him what he had wanted for his birthday, he told me that he had already got his wish! He had wished for me to come home for his birthday.

CHAPTER NINE

Home Sweet Home

As a great inner calm started to slowly pervade my life, I begin to feel a sense of joyous exhilaration that I had not known for some time. I began to feel increasingly more at home in my own skin and outer world that had been so abruptly turned upside down ...

$\mathcal{B}$y the time I went home, the pancreatitis and pneumonia had subsided. Even though the blood clots in my veins had not yet completely resolved, I had managed to develop an adequate collateral flow subsequent to the clot formation. As a result, I was put on a strict regime of blood thinners, antibiotics and oral hypoglycemics that required close monitoring by my family physician. I also needed to be under specialist care for the next several months following my discharge from hospital.

When I left the Peter Lougheed Center after spending nearly two months in hospital, I felt like a walking dispensary accompanied as I was with my caseload of pills, crutches, walker and a wad of detailed instructions to follow. Even though I was able to make it home under my own steam, I was not quite ready to turn cartwheels yet. However, the *Welcome Home* banner lovingly prepared by my family that greeted me at the front door brought a lump to my throat, making me want to jump for joy. I realized then, that home is truly where the heart is.

By now the memory of my 'experience' was beginning to fade. Just as a newborn babe freshly arrived from the spirit world begins to forget its spiritual origins as it gets acclimatized to its physical environment, so did I. And by the time I left the four walls and domain of the hospital that had been my home for the last several weeks, the memory of where I had been had already started to glaze over in my mind. Even though I still had a general overall impression of the experience, the finer details from the experience were beginning to get sketchy and obscure like some fragmented dream.

Before long, I had fallen victim to the 'veil of forgetfulness' that falls imperceptibly over you like a dark and heavy curtain. The 'forgetting,' I realized, was for my own good. It helped me to some extent preserve and safeguard my sanity by allowing me to function more fully in the moment. Consequently, the memory of my past lives was not allowed to interfere or get in the way of my present life.

This forgetting or amnesia, I discovered, is Nature's way of giving each of us a fresh start in life. In fact, each of us stood a better chance of fulfilling our individual missions of growth if we were unencumbered by our pasts, and not constantly judging others or ourselves for errors or omissions committed in the past. The trouble often began when memories from our past lives started to involuntarily surface and impinge upon our present consciousness — as in the case of persons suffering from a multiple personality disorder.

Although there seems to be a real basis to this dissociative disorder, it is a bewildering condition that causes one to lose touch with his or her present reality. In losing this critical mental control, we essentially become impotent in our lives. We are unable to take advantage of the opportunities for growth and self-development in our *current* lives — which is one of the main reasons for our being on Earth.

Therefore, in my case, I personally felt it fortuitous that I was beginning to forget as it made it easier for me to get on with my life and focus on getting better. Besides, I felt my case was not all that unique and I certainly was not the first, nor would I be the last, to survive clinical death. As I recall, even Plato, the ancient Greek philosopher who lived in Athens from 428-348 B.C., had made reference to this same phenomenon centuries before in several of his philosophical works. More notably, in his Book X of *The Republic* he relates the tale of a Greek soldier (in the *Myth of Er*) who returns from a funeral pyre several days after dying on the battlefield, and talks emphatically of an afterlife and visiting other planes of existence.

Moreover, I have to admit that talking openly about my near-death experience was not something that I would have volunteered anyway, even if my memory had not started to fade. There was always that fear of being judged or ridiculed by people who did not understand. Besides, the experience itself was of such an intensely personal nature that I felt it was something I needed to savor and reflect upon in the privacy of my own mind, as opposed to offering it for general consumption. Therefore, under the circumstances, I was quite willing to forget it all and just chalk it up to experience.

But as I was quick to discover, that was not to be. The very next day after being discharged from hospital, I recall hearing the doorbell ring around suppertime. It was not the pizza deliveryman standing at my doorstep, but my sister and a woman in her fifties from Montreal who called herself a 'light worker.' Apparently, she had heard of my near-death encounter from my sister who had just completed a two-day workshop with her, and had come to pay me a visit. And one of the first things she said to me was that she had been sent to me by God, to help break the 'veil of forgetfulness' that had already begun to form around me!

Although this sounded strange and a little over the top even for me, and quite possibly a clever ploy on her part to persuade me to take her 'Emotions Workshop,' I decided to hear her out more out of politeness than anything else. But by the end of the six hours or so that she was there, I realized that I was the one doing most of the talking as opposed to the other way around. She had deftly taken me back to the first moment of my experience, pressing me for detail here and there and, in the process, helping me draw out some of the half-forgotten details of my experience.

Even though I was not able to quite fully resurrect the experience in its entirety, I did, nevertheless, end up taking the 'Emotions Workshop' with her over the course of the next few days that followed. My sole reason for taking the workshop was to explore the 'emotional' basis for some of the physical ills in my life. From what I gathered, it was a matter of identifying and *consciously* acknowledging the pent-up emotions in my life, and then releasing the emotions that I may subconsciously be holding onto since childhood. The whole idea behind this 'emotional off-loading' was to aid my physical recovery, and was the kind of metaphysical 'mind over matter' stuff that I was just beginning to buy into.

The main area of focus in the workshop was to help me isolate my emotional fears and let go of any anger or resentment that I was still holding onto in my life. I discovered that fear, as well as anger and other negative emotions that we harbor in our hearts, have a tendency to manifest themselves physically in our bodies. Also, contrary to popular belief — guilt, remorse and regret, actually carried a potential for great good in our lives. They provided that vital inner tug and emotional motivation in our lives that compelled us to do the 'right' thing by making amends for our past mistakes, and in the process slowly reform ourselves.

However, something that I had not expected was to spontaneously regress *beyond* the point of my present life, and go into a tirade of emotions from my *past* lives! As several of my past lives began to flash before me, one that absolutely stood out for me was life as a Roman soldier. From what I could make out, I had cruelly denied water to some thirsty wayfarers trekking their way east under the hot desert sun during what appeared to be biblical times.

In that single flash of recognition, I was able to make perfect sense of my recent predicament in hospital where I was made to undergo forty days without water. The 'law of karma' — or that biblical notion of an eye for an eye, and a tooth for a tooth, had unerringly caught up with me. I could now see exactly how I was made to atone for my *past* cruelty by getting a taste of my own medicine in my *present* life.

Although it is not something that I am proud of, it nevertheless served to demonstrate to me that none of us are born perfect, and that whoever said we only lived once was sadly mistaken. I also saw how we have clearly had to evolve from hard-hearted barbarians — who constantly trampled on human rights, into the somewhat more enlightened human beings of today through the process of refinement and the endless recycling of our souls.

Thus, one of the most profound realizations I made here was that life is ultimately a matter of 'improving' ourselves. It is a matter of cultivating that precious thing called *conscience* — or that ability to discern 'right' from 'wrong,' during the course of our many lifetimes on earth. And it is only through the process of making amends, by righting our wrongs and learning from our past mistakes, that we can finally get off that seemingly endless cycle of reincarnation.

I further discovered that the qualities of mercy, kindness, sharing, caring and compassion for others, are qualities that we essentially have to acquire through actual life experiences. It is something that we all have to learn on the job so to speak, as we go through *several* rounds of life on this school of 'hard-knocks' called Earth. So, whether we liked it or not, or chose to believe in the process or not, we were inextricably bound to our physical globe in chains. And until such time as we had earned the right to emancipate ourselves from those karmic chains — one slow and painful link at a time, we were forever destined to be a part of that vicious cycle of birth and rebirth known as 'reincarnation.'

* * *

Reaching *beyond* the span of my current life, I was told, was actually not that common. As far as I am aware, it was not something that any of the other participants in the workshop seemed to have experienced. Recalling past life information, nevertheless, was just an added bonus for me in my quest for the truth. The highlight of the workshop for me, however, came not from this fascinating foray into my past lives, but what subsequently transpired in a meditation session at the end of the two-day workshop.

I recall clearing my breath and slowly losing myself to the silence. I do not know how long I remained in that state of surrender, but I remember finding myself in the presence of a brilliant white Light that seemed to come out of nowhere. Even as I recognized it to be the shining countenance of my Lord, I found myself being compellingly drawn into the Light. It seemed like I had somehow managed to reconnect with the *same* Light that I had encountered at death — except that this time around I was alive and breathing, and fully cognizant of the fact!

As I penetrated the dispersing mists of my oblivion, I found myself getting rapidly drawn into a reality in which I felt increasingly at home. Vaguely at first, and then more clearly, all the fascinating little details from my so-called 'experience' came flooding back into my mind. That which had become obscured was once again revealed, as I found myself slipping effortlessly into the next dimension.

I was elated. I had managed to pierce through the 'veil of forgetfulness' via the age-old art of meditation and transported myself back Home. By focusing and concentrating the scattered ray of my mind onto my third eye, I had managed to burn a tiny hole in the existing mantle of my consciousness. And to my great astonishment, I found myself looking at the *same* reality that I had encountered during the undeniably more grueling process of my near-death experience.

Even as I reached the threshold of my realization, I felt myself disengage from this all-pervading Light of love, knowledge and wisdom. I knew then, beyond the slightest shadow of a doubt, that my present experience was not the result of some hallucinogenic drug weaving its fanciful magic upon my mind but the detached observations of a fully conscious mind. And I realized then that, whichever way you looked at it, the physical act of 'dying' was a *spiritual* experience, and that meditation was an infinitely easier way to experience one's death.

In that moment of crystal clarity, I saw that what we refer to as 'death' is really a grand and magnificent *awakening*, and that point of highest consciousness in an individual soul. Also, meditation, I discovered, is by far the more predictable way of moving on to the next level of consciousness and engaging in the dynamics of a higher reality — while we were still *alive*. In other words, one does not necessarily have to be pronounced clinically dead in order to undergo the 'dying' experience.

I, thus, made a profound realization. In order to participate in the dying process and become a part of an altered consciousness, one does not have to withdraw from life or travel through space in a physical sense. What is required is a mental and, to some extent, an emotional detachment from our physical bodies. This can happen voluntarily as in the case of someone in a meditative trance, or involuntarily — as in the case of someone in a coma or someone, like myself, undergoing a near-death experience.

Technically, what is required is the stilling of one's mind in order to experience an 'out-of-body' state that allows our consciousness to travel to other less physical dimensions of being. In fact, it is something that occurs quite naturally every night in our sleep. But because it happens involuntarily and at a subconscious level, it is not something that we tend to pay a lot of attention to or, indeed, have a lucid recollection of, during our waking moments of consciousness. So to refer to sleep as a 'mini-death,' and death as a brother or second cousin to 'sleep,' is actually closer to the mark than we think.

* * *

Catching a glimpse of the greater reality behind the façade of my ordinary life in meditation went a long way towards helping me reconcile myself to life again. However, trying to get back to the business of living was not easy. I remember getting cautiously out of bed the next day and feeling like I had been hit by a two-ton truck. I felt 'shell-shocked,' dazed, and literally sick to my stomach. I felt totally drained and emotionally empty inside. I even began to question whether taking the 'Emotions Workshop' had been a wise move on my part, and honestly wondered whether I would ever regain my strength.

So when Judith, the person who had facilitated the workshop, called me the next day, urging me to get some fresh air and to start putting down on paper some of the details from my 'experience,' I flat out refused. Writing was the farthest thing from my mind. I had neither the will nor the inclination to write. All I wanted to do was to focus on regaining my strength and getting my life back on track. And so the harder she tried to convince me — even reminding me that I had been specifically entrusted with the task of writing this book, the longer I stalled and rebelled against the very idea of it.

Unlike my last book on the Judge, I just did not seem to have that inner drive to write. I knew from personal experience that the motivation to write was something that had to come from within, as opposed to someone else prompting me to write. So until such time as I felt that inner drive to write, I could not see myself writing convincingly about a subject that, theoretically, I didn't know a hell of a lot about. Besides, it was such a subjective experience that even talking about it would be to leave myself wide open to criticism from those who believed that some things were just too sacred to talk about, and were best left unsaid.

Despite this inner conflict in my head, I did, nevertheless manage to get physically stronger. My progress, however, came in baby steps where each step forward felt like a small milestone in my life. I clearly remember the day when I was able to swallow my first steak dinner, something that I could not do before due to the long length of time I had been on a ventilator and feeding tube. That blessed day turned out to be Valentine's Day which, among other things, also marked the completion of my six-week-long course of antibiotics.

The next high point in my life came when I was able to graduate from using a pair of crutches, to a walker, and then finally my own two feet. Being able to walk on my own after more than two months in bed definitely spelled freedom for me. But the real moment of truth came three months later in May, when I was completely weaned off the blood thinners. As anticipated, the blood clots in my veins did finally resolve. My blood sugar and enzyme levels, too, were back within a normal range, and I certainly felt ready to kick up my heels and party.

Curiously, a chance remark by Dr. Valentine — the blood specialist monitoring my progress at the Foothills Hospital in Calgary, somehow struck a chord. Although she was, of course, delighted at the fortunate outcome of my case, she openly admitted that it had not looked quite so good the day she first saw me in hospital. She also confessed that she believed in divine intervention, and often saw terminally ill patients in her practice. Writing about my experience, she felt, could have a positive impact on her patients and others like them by helping them overcome their fear of dying.

* * *

In any event I was now off the danger list, and by the end of June was strong enough to take a short trip east with the family. I was eager to see the world again with what felt like 'new' eyes. With less of the potent drugs coursing through my veins, I felt a certain clarity of feeling and being that is hard to describe. The world and everything in it somehow appeared brighter and more vibrant than before. Colors looked more vivid and alive, and there was an intriguing aura of freshness and crispness surrounding everything I saw. I even seemed to hear music an octave or two higher than I did before. But more than hearing the music, I *felt* it in my soul. All my senses seemed sharper and keener, and I even seemed to have a heightened perception of events and their outcome.

In short, all my senses sang and rejoiced as I found myself becoming increasingly more receptive to all the beauty and marvel of life that surrounded me. Even though outwardly everything appeared to be the same, something *inside* me had inexplicably changed. It was as though the very essence of who I was had been 'reconfigured' or transformed as a result of my encounter with the Light. Not only did I look at life differently, but I also seemed to be *reacting* differently to the same old dramas and situations in my life. Incredibly, I felt more alive than I did before. It was as though I somehow possessed more 'soul' than I did before.

The downside of feeling all this joy, however, was that I

also felt the pain and sorrow in my life that much more acutely than I did before. I felt myself becoming increasingly more sensitive to the violence and suffering that abounded in the world. So while my happiness at being alive knew no bounds, the pain I felt inside seemed almost too excruciating for words. I felt profoundly shaken to the core as I watched the daily brutality of world events unfold around me.

So even though I had spent one of the most wonderful summers on record, there were days when I found myself lying awake in bed at night, silently crying myself to sleep. There were also times when I felt like an outsider inside my own home, alienated from a world that seemed oblivious to the pain and torment in my heart. The next several months following my discharge from hospital were some of the hardest to live through. There were indeed times when I questioned the sanity of my decision to return to a cynical world and houseful of insurgent teenage hormones, which further added to my sense of isolation and disconnection.

As I struggled to conceal the open wound of my pain, it became evident that in order to survive in a world that now seemed suddenly harsher and more cruel, I needed to take some affirmative action in my life. I knew that I would have to reach into the innermost reaches of my soul and find some way of desensitizing myself against the rising tide of discontent in my heart.

Shielding my pain with a mask of indifference helped to temporarily ward off the pinpricks of pain ripping into my soul. While I recognized the need for a more permanent solution to this inner turmoil in my heart, I knew it was something that I would essentially have to come to terms with myself. Although professional counseling did help me put things into their proper perspective, deep down in my heart I knew that I needed to take a vastly different approach to life itself.

Surprisingly enough, I found the answer right inside the privacy of my own home. Every time I found myself slipping into that dark hole of despair, I would remind myself of the immense joy and happiness that I had experienced in the other realm — something that could never be erased from my heart. Before long, I found myself naturally reflecting upon the calm and tranquility of my inner world in meditation. And slowly but surely, the outward disturbances in my life no longer seemed to have the power to shake or perturb that immutable inner core of my being. I had found my inner calm and peace in meditation.

* * *

I have to admit that I had some help finding this inner resource within myself. For some reason, ever since being discharged from hospital, I would find myself being aroused from sleep between the early morning hours of 3:00 and 5:00 each morning. Rather than let my mind wander, I decided to use that time constructively by consciously stilling that 'empty chatter' in my mind through meditation.

I can remember being awakened from an unusually deep sleep one morning, while still in that in-between state of wakefulness and sleep, by a quaint little Shakespearian or

Elizabethan phrase that kept repeating itself over and over in my mind. The strange phrase *"Prepare thyself to receive"* kept being drummed into my head for the next couple of days straight, around more or less the same time each morning.

Although I initially dismissed it as just another 'dream,' a curious incident later on in the year abruptly changed my mind. I remember waking up to the delicate sound of chimes towards the end of August, around 3:30 in the morning. It was one of the most exquisite sounds I had heard that not only splintered my silence, but also the entire right side of my body! The top of my head right down to the tip of my toes seemed to be on fire. I began to feel a warm tingling sensation and powerful rush of energy course through my right arm and the entire right side of my body. Yet, for some strange reason, the left side of my body remained wholly unaffected by this electrifying surge of energy.

My first impression was that I was perhaps having a stroke! Even as I struggled with the very idea of it, an incredible calm and clarity of purpose began to come over me. As realization upon realization began to heap upon my mind, words, chapter headings and whole sentences began to flow rapidly into my head. I do not know how long this surreal moment lasted, but it was long enough to convince me of what it was that I had to do. I knew then that I had to write this book in the format that had just been revealed to me.

After months of agonizing over the decision of whether or not to write this book, I felt that I had finally received a sign that I simply could not ignore. It felt as 'real' to me as the near-death experience itself. Even though verbally communicating my experience to others still went against the very grain of my being, I felt I had no choice but to write this book. I now felt absolutely driven to write this book, in the same way that I had felt compelled to write my last book on the Judge. I knew it was something that I *had* to do, and was no longer something I could deliberately turn my back on.

* * *

By early September, my life was finally starting to get back on an even keel. The boys were back in school for the start of the academic year, and I now seemed to have more time on my hands. Even though it was still very hard for me to talk about my experience, I felt this urgent need to commit to paper some of the more salient points from my experience while still relatively fresh in my mind. But as I began to make rough notes from memory, something quite remarkable started to unravel in my head. Ideas, concepts and theories started to form frantically in my mind. They began to flow faster than I could physically put them down on paper.

What seemed strange was not the spontaneity of the writing process, but the fact that the very nature of thought being transmitted was something that had, until then, been quite foreign to my understanding of life itself. Except for my own vague and generalized notions of life — and death, I seemed to have little control over what was coming through my *pen*.

After approximately six weeks of this relentless outpouring of ideas, the writing came to an abrupt halt. With it also came a profound sense of peace and release. It was as though

I had finally laid to rest an intensely disquieting bee in my bonnet, and the whole weight of the world had suddenly been lifted from my shoulders.

As I continued to meditate, even if only for minutes each day, I discovered that I had found that elusive key with which to keep myself calm and grounded. It not only helped to anesthetize my pain and allay my fears of the task that I knew lay ahead, but it also helped me overcome that sense of extreme restlessness in my life. As a great inner calm started to slowly pervade my life, I began to feel a sense of joyous exhilaration that I had not known for some time. I began to feel increasingly more at home in my own skin and the outer world that I lived in. And when people remarked that it must have been *hell* to have so narrowly escaped death, I could casually reply: "*Well, some people actually call that heaven.*"

CHAPTER TEN

Reflections of a Dreamer

There were times when I questioned the validity of my own experience, and even wondered if I had perhaps dreamed it all up. And in order to seek out my truth, I knew I would have to ask myself that tough question: 'Was it all a magnificent dream or the grandest reality that I was ever likely to encounter?'

*I*n expressing on paper that which I could not verbally articulate, my mind felt suddenly relieved of all its clutter. I found myself thinking with a greater clarity and objectivity than I did before. And as the left side of my brain slowly started to take over, I found myself systematically breaking down and analyzing some of the more puzzling aspects of my so-called 'experience.'

One of the things that had perplexed me ever since taking the Emotions Workshop was the ability to rattle off my past lives like as though it were yesterday's news. Even though I realized that those lives belonged firmly in the past, and could in no way impinge upon my present life, to have spontaneously dredged up a memory of them in a fully conscious and non-hypnotized state did not seem quite normal to me. At the same time, I did not have any problem seeing myself reflected in the faces of my many personalities from the past, as I genuinely believed in reincarnation and the vital role that it played in our growth process.

So while the memory of my past lives was not causing confusion in my life as such, there were certain aspects of it that were beginning to wear on me intellectually. What had puzzled me the most were those persistent flashes of memory in which I saw myself as an *inanimate* rock, as well as a magnificent horse in flight. Things just did not seem to add up in my mind, and there were, indeed, times when I questioned the validity of my own experience and even wondered if I had perhaps dreamed it all up. So long as I had questions in my mind that remained unanswered, I knew I would not rest — let alone write a book on the whole baffling process of life after death.

In fact, my eleven-year-old son, Shafin, had posed virtually the same question to me in all the guileless innocence of his youth. He had simply asked, *"How do you know it wasn't a dream?"* I realized then that he had unwittingly summed up what other people were perhaps thinking, but could not quite say to my face. There was, however, one woman in her fifties who did make an oblique reference to it by asking me how could I have possibly "seen" this other world when my eyes were closed and I was supposedly in a coma!

Although I tried explaining to her that it was like seeing yourself in a very clear and lucid dream, where you visualized and experienced the dream in spite of the fact that your eyes were physically closed, I knew she was not convinced. Yet, it was queries such as these that helped strengthen my resolve to investigate more fully into the phenomenon of near-death experiences. It soon became clear to me that my task in the final analysis was not to convince her or anybody else — but to convince *myself*.

As a writer and journalist, I knew that to be able to write convincingly with some measure of credibility, I needed to be objective and keep myself emotionally detached from my writing. This meant that I would not only have to seek out facts as they pertained to near-death experiences in general, but I would also have to use reason and intellectual argument to establish a sound basis for my own 'truth.'

There are, of course, some questions that are just too important not to be asked. And I realized that, arguably, I would have to be the first to question my own experience. I would, in effect, have to take on the role of devil's advocate and argue the case *against* my own highly personal experience in death and what lay beyond. Indeed, I would have to ask myself that tough question, "*Was it all a magnificent dream or the grandest reality that I was ever likely to encounter?*"

By now I was absolutely convinced in my heart that what I had experienced was real, and not some fantastic dream. It had felt as real to me as anything that I had seen, felt, heard or touched. Yet, there was still that inborn skeptic in me that clamored for logic and refused to take things at face value. I felt this deep-rooted need to rationalize the experience in my own mind, and figure out for myself whether or not it was all a product of an over-active imagination — or something infinitely more real.

Therefore, before I could find some measure of peace within myself, I felt the need to *intellectually* satisfy myself that what I had, in fact, encountered was an alternate reality that existed alongside my present reality. And so, one of the first legitimate points of inquiry to myself was, "*If it had, indeed, been a 'dream,' how was it possible for so many of us to have dreamt fundamentally the same dream at a point in our lives when clinical death seemed imminent?*"

Oddly enough, it was precisely this line of questioning or 'dialectic inquiry' — namely, using reason and logic to arrive at the truth, that finally led me to embrace my own truth. It made me realize that the answer to my original question of whether or not it was a dream, perhaps lay in scrutinizing the nature and content of my *other* dreams. Through the process of analyzing my dreams, I felt there was a good chance that I would be able to see for myself exactly how well my particular recollections of 'death' stacked up to those dreams.

* * *

In recalling several of my dreams, which in the past had subtly pointed me towards the truth, I was surprised to learn that I actually had a long and recurring history of dreams that *had* come true. I had just assumed that the precognitive or prophetic element in my dreams was a genetic trait that I had inherited from the maternal side of my family, and was something that I had always taken for granted.

However, it was not until I was about eighteen years old that I first became aware of the relevance of the dreaming process. It was around the time that my father had passed away unexpectedly without leaving behind a will. A situation subsequently arose where it became crucial that his will — if it existed, or a business lease at least, be located as my family was faced with a very real possibility of forfeiting a profitable family business that my father had personally helped revive. Then, at what seemed like the eleventh hour, my father had appeared to my mother in a dream advising her of the whereabouts of the lease as well as the missing will. The lease was found the next day in a little-used safe, and the will was discovered in the offices of a certain lawyer — exactly as my father had indicated in the dream!

In casting my mind back to the first time that I personally had experienced such a dream, I realized there was no 'first' time. It was something I thought everyone did as a child. It was only as I grew older that I realized that seeing glimpses of the future being projected in your dreams was not all that common. In any event, I continued to dream my insignificant little dreams, which for all intents and purposes had little or no impact on my life. Although my dreams were not exactly earth-shattering in themselves, events in my day-to-day life did, however, seem strangely familiar. It was like experiencing *déjà vu* or a re-run of an incident that I had already 'seen' before.

Upon a closer scrutiny of my dreams, I realized that most

of my dreams — whether of consequence or not, seemed to specifically hint at some *future* event imminent in my own life, or the life of someone close to me. I could vividly recall such a time many years ago, when I had casually asked a friend if he had found the bicycle that he was looking for. He seemed surprised that I should ask him that as he had not mentioned it to anyone. I had, nevertheless, 'seen' it quite clearly in a dream just days before.

Then there was also the time when I had seen a troop of monkeys scampering about in my dream on top of what looked like a Hindu temple — a sight that is not typical of the rooftops of North America. As it turned out, it was not a part of my imagination but a *real* temple that still exists a whole continent away in Zambia, in the city of Lusaka! It was a part of Africa that I had never been to before, but had subsequently visited within two months of that dream.

I have always shared a special connection with my sister, Faiza, who had lived abroad in Tripoli, Libya, for many years before relocating with her family to St. John's, Newfoundland. Even though I never managed to physically visit her at any of those places, I was often able to describe the layout of some of the houses that she had lived in, or was contemplating buying, through my dreams. I could often describe to her the surrounding landscape, including certain structural defects — such as a crack in the wall, and occasionally the view outside. I even recall describing to a friend that she had introduced me to, the view outside a particular window and a shortcut to a certain mosque in Dar-es-Salaam, Tanzania — in spite of the fact that I have yet to set foot in that town.

Clearly, time or distance did not seem to be an obstacle in

my dreams. In fact, I remember seeing myself in Toronto in a dream one time *before* such a trip was contemplated. As it turned out, I did take a spur-of-the-moment trip to Toronto that same year and had stayed in a house that I had 'seen' in a suburb of Toronto that I had never been to before. What was curious was the fact that I recalled having some difficulty negotiating a certain step leading to the main entrance of the house in that dream. During my actual trip to Toronto, the middle step to the front entrance of the house was, indeed, very wobbly — something that our hosts had apparently only noticed a day or two before we arrived.

Several years before that, I had foreseen the funeral of a certain relative living in eastern Canada in a very specific dream, in which I had seen my brother act as a pallbearer. The relation in question had died unexpectedly, around the time that my brother just happened to be visiting Canada.

A few years ago, I remember bidding farewell to a close friend of the family in a dream — in spite of the fact that I had spoken to him on the phone only hours before, and was planning to visit him in Las Vegas over Christmas. He had been struggling with cancer during the last few years of his life and, as it turned out, had gone into a coma shortly after we had spoken on the phone. He passed away on Christmas Day before I got a chance to speak to him again.

More recently, I remember dreaming that the credit cards being mailed to us had been given a fresh new look, and that the original color had been changed to gray. In the same dream, I had also 'seen' those cards being intercepted at the point of mailing. A few days later, we got a phone call from our bank advising us to destroy any cards that we received in the mail subsequent to their phone call, as they were in the process of re-issuing our credit cards. When we finally did receive the new cards, they were in the same shade of gray as I had envisioned in my dream. Interestingly enough, we also received a set of similar looking credit cards in the mail a week later — in an envelope that looked like it had been obviously steamed open and tampered with.

Apart from the ordinary, run-of-the-mill, garden variety type of dreams that at the end of the day did not amount to much, there were also dreams that have had a major impact on my life. In looking back, I realized that there have been several key or pivotal moments in my life that have occurred subsequent to some mysterious hint or vision that had come to me by way of a dream. Although I generally tended to dismiss my dreams as a way for my subconscious to process and clear away its daily clutter, I realized, in retrospect, that there were definitely times when my dreams had provided me with an invaluable insight into my future.

Specifically, I remember the time when my father-in-law, who had passed away some thirty years before, had appeared to me in a vivid dream giving me his blessing to marry his son. Although the question of marriage had seemed a little premature at the time, I, nevertheless, did marry Amin a few months later. The strange part was that I had never laid eyes on my father-in-law before then. In fact, I had never even seen a photograph of him. Yet, I was able to describe him to Amin in accurate detail, both in his demeanor and personality, right down to the kind of footwear he liked to wear.

Then there was also notably the time when my Lord had appeared to me in an exceptionally vivid dream, emphatically reminding me that mine was the hand of a writer — long before writing professionally had entered my mind. As it turned out, I did graduate in journalism and publish my first book within six years of that dream.

But the one dream that has had the greatest impact on my life was the time when I had seen myself gasping for breath and drown whilst on holiday. Incredibly, only five months later, in December of 1998, I had actually stopped breathing as a result of respiratory failure and experienced my own 'death' whilst vacationing in Florida. What was remarkable about this last dream was the fact that I had somehow managed to cross-over into a totally *different* plane of reality — one that had seemed strangely familiar to me during my *actual* brush with death.

I remember being greeted by deceased members of my family in that dream, who had informed me that I was 'dead' and no longer a part of the physical world. Remarkably, it was recalling those very same words, along with the over-whelming familiarity of my venue during my actual brush with death that had instantly awoken me to the truth. It had unequivocally driven home to me the fact that what I was experiencing was *not* a dream, but the real thing.

So, yes, dreams I could certainly believe in. In fact, there have been times in my life when I have set greater store by what I have 'seen' in my dreams than what may otherwise seem more logical to assume. There are usually no false façades or hidden agendas to contend with in my dreams, as what I see is generally what I get. Therefore, clairvoyant dreams as such have always had a legitimate place in my realm of probability as well as experience.

As Henry David Thoreau — someone who looked to natural phenomena for the truth, reminded us, *"Our truest life is when we are in dreams awake."* Hence, a lucid, clearly remembered dream that did not resemble a jumbled up sequence of events could, to my mind, well provide us with an invaluable roadmap into the more hidden and unseen dimensions of our lives.

If, on the off-chance, my near-death experience was a 'dream' — one that had taken me past the corridors of death and beyond, then given my past experience with dreams, there was a good possibility that it, too, *could* be a valid precursor to 'death' itself. At the very least, I recognized that my 'dreamlike' experience with death had provided me with a 'window' into a whole new world that I would not otherwise have known. It made me realize that dreams certainly held the potential of being a gateway to a much wider and broader range of experience that went far beyond the physical.

* * *

Through the process of consciously analyzing my dreams, I was thus able to personally verify for myself — with some degree of accuracy, many of the events that had transpired in my life subsequent to those dreams. But whether or not I understood the whole mysterious process of dreaming was irrelevant. What was relevant was the fact that I always seemed to come back to my present reality with *some* material piece of information of which I had no prior knowledge, but which later turned out to be true.

Moreover, it was not the type of information that one could easily access in the normal or conventional manner, such as through textbooks, the internet, or our high-speed information technologies of today. It was information that grabbed you and struck you like a bolt of lightning, instantly changing your perspective on life. But more than that, it was *felt* knowledge that you experienced — as in the case of an exceptionally vivid dream, where you both felt and experienced the events in your dream.

This systematic investigation into my dreams prompted me to pay closer attention to some of the seemingly absurd details in my nocturnal forays into the astral world. Besides, having personally witnessed some very specific events unfold in my life subsequent to those dreams, made me realize that life was not comprised of a series of 'random' events that occurred on the spur of the moment. Instead, it was made up of 'planned' events that happened by design and a reasonable degree of predictability in our lives.

Therefore, if my near-death experience turned out to be an inspired 'dream,' which contained information that could possibly be true, then it was something I felt deserved a second look. The challenge for me personally lay in making greater sense of my 'dreamlike' experience — one that I seemed to recall in such clear and mesmerizing detail. So before I could in all good conscience dismiss my experience as just another 'dream,' I felt I owed it to myself to at least seek out information that could well corroborate my truth.

* * *

Verifying the earlier 'out-of-body' phase of my experience proved to be relatively easy. I found several well-documented accounts of people that had undergone similar experiences who described going through 'a tunnel' and meeting their loved ones, before being subjected to a 'life review.' Some even went as far as describing an encounter with a bright 'white light' which they recognized as being that of their Lord and Savior.

Trying to find documentation that supported my claim of encountering a rarefied world of light without color, feature or form, however, was harder to come by. I, nevertheless, felt this overwhelming need to intellectually examine and pursue *every* anomaly, or seemingly obvious deviation from the norm in my experience, before dismissing my search altogether.

I find it is human nature to reject out of hand that which does not fit in quite so neatly into our compartmentalized notions of reality by the analytical and cognitive portions of our brain. Therefore, in order to prevent myself from committing the cardinal sin of losing the baby with the bath water, I felt compelled to keep an open mind and literally think 'outside the box.' This meant that I would not only have to engage in conventional research, but probe deeper into my own subconscious as well as the hidden and more metaphysical aspects of my life.

Although there is no substitute for inner experience, I still felt this overwhelming need for some kind of *external* validation in order for me to come to terms with my own experience. Consequently, in an effort to reconcile myself to my near-death experience or the 'truth' as I perceived it, I found myself being drawn into a fact-finding mission of sorts that dominated the next three years of my life. And it was only during the course of this fascinating round of research — which included, among other things, philosophy, theosophy, mythology, religion, and aspects of my own spiritual tradition, that I was finally able to substantiate my truth.

The mainstay of my research had revolved mainly around searching for information that either confirmed my experience, or alluded to a similar experience. Fortunately for me, the often cumbersome and frustrating task of locating and comparing information that supported my own claims proved easier than I had first supposed. Books on a wide variety of subjects started to magically appear by my bedside as family and well-meaning friends began to recommend, or drop-off, books that they felt might be of interest to me.

Even though I had not been a particularly avid reader of New Age or spiritual literature up until then, I knew that in order to seek out my truth it was not an avenue I could afford to ignore. To my great astonishment, even before I became conscious of it, I found myself being immersed and thoroughly captivated by the information contained in these books. And as everything slowly started to make sense, I was finally able to piece together the missing pieces of the subliminal puzzle floating around in my head.

* * *

Incredibly, I realized with a sense of profound wonder that in my quest for the truth, I had uncovered what in essence had lain dormant in my backyard all along. My search had brought me unerringly back to my own spiritual roots — namely, *Sathpanth Ismailism* and that mystical branch of Islam known as Sufism.

As a Shia Ismaili Muslim whose East Indian forefathers had been converted to Islam from Hinduism during the 11th century, a certain strain of eastern mysticism still persisted in my brand of spiritual philosophy. Remarkably, I discovered that it was from this pool of collective wisdom that I had drawn my 'spiritual sap' without actually being aware of it.

I realized that I had come full circle. But it was not until I started to seriously research Eastern religions and Islamic literature composed by the great Sufi mystics and Persian poets like Jalal al-Din Rumi, Omar Khayyam, Hafiz, Attar and Nasir Khusraw, that I began to gain a deeper understanding into my own spiritual make up. I was surprised to learn that both Eastern and Islamic doctrine — my *own* faith, have always acknowledged the existence of spirit, soul or that spark of the divine in ALL things, from the minutest particle of matter — whether vegetable, animal or mineral, to the elements and space itself.

This *animist* view of life — where everything in the cosmos or Universe, whether alive or inert, is animated by a living consciousness and energy, is thought to be the earliest type of spiritualism practiced by humans. Rumi, the 13th century Sufi mystic and poet, takes this concept a step further in his *Mathnawi* — 'Rhymed Couplets of Deep Spiritual Meaning,' as translated by A.J. Arberry:

> *"I died as a mineral and became a plant,*
> *I died as plant and rose to animal,*
> *I died as animal and I was Man.*
> *Why should I fear? When was I less by dying?*
> *Yet once more I shall die as Man, to soar with angels*
> *But even from angelhood I must pass on*
> *All except God shall perish ..."*

Rumi's insightful description of the progression of the soul, or that spark of the divine in us, helped me recognize our innate interconnectedness to *all* levels of existence, both animate *and* inanimate. Remarkably, it dawned upon me that being a part of this 'unified consciousness' was something I had actually experienced myself. This helped further reinforce the fact that we are all really a part of the *same* whole.

More importantly, what had first seemed ludicrous and perhaps the most difficult part of my experience to digest — namely, my vivid recollections as an *inanimate* rock, a free-spirited horse and a gyrating dolphin, now seemed suddenly plausible in the eyes of one of the great mystics of our time! It, therefore, stood to reason that whatever else I might have had trouble accepting, too, could have a hidden element or kernel of truth just waiting to be thrashed out and exposed.

I now started to see my near-death experience in a whole new light. Yet, when it came to scrutinizing the so-called 'mythical' element in my experience, it still continued to pose a serious challenge for me. I knew I would have to draw a strict line between what was deemed pure myth or legend, and what was considered historical fact. Therefore, trying to justify the majestic vision of a two-headed Zeus, the Greek God of gods, standing shoulder to shoulder with Amon-Ra, the mythological sun god and Egyptian deity revered as the King of gods was, I felt, perhaps stretching it a bit.

However, almost a year after my near-death incident, I accidentally stumbled onto a tantalizing piece of information whilst flipping channels on television that made me sit up and take notice. I was absolutely flabbergasted to learn that, according to legend, the Greek god Zeus actually did appear to have *two* heads at one point when he purportedly gave birth to his daughter Athena through his forehead, after swallowing the Titaness Metis! It made me wonder how I could have possibly conjured up a 'two-headed' image of Zeus when I had not, even remotely, been aware of the prevailing myth surrounding Zeus and his daughter, Athena.

Stumbling upon this fascinating piece of information prompted me to re-evaluate and examine more closely what I had been 'shown' in the spirit world. As I delved deeper into Greek and Egyptian mythology, I was surprised to learn that both Zeus and Amon-Ra were considered chief deities and universal gods in their own right. In fact, Zeus was frequently identified with the Egyptian God, Amon-Ra — whose name meant 'The Hidden One,' and whose authority extended far beyond that of Egypt alone. Moreover, both had, at one time or another, been linked to and identified with the legendary Roman god, Jupiter.

Finding this common link between two seemingly unrelated 'heavyweights' in the world of mythology, and having 'seen' them standing shoulder to shoulder without being aware of their equal ranking, certainly gave me food for thought. It made me question whether my seeing the two of them together was a mere 'coincidence,' or a contrived event specially staged to help open my eyes to some greater truth that had thus far eluded me.

I even started to wonder whether there was perhaps a grain of truth in what we popularly dismissed as myth or legend. And I seriously began to question whether history as we know it has to be physically recorded, or scientifically proven, in order for it to be accepted as historical fact — even though mighty civilizations had fallen and risen *long before* we started to record that which we call 'history.'

* * *

The myths surrounding Zeus and Amon-Ra could, for all intents and purposes, be considered the stuff of legend and, therefore, suspect. But I realized that there were other recognizable figures in the group that had formed a part of my living history — such as Mahatma Gandhi or Martin Luther King, Jr., both of whom I had recognized immediately. But trying to put a name to the faces of *Mira Behn* and Chief Crowfoot, individuals whom I had heard of but never laid eyes on, was much slower in coming. It was not until several months later that I was able to positively identify the two.

Curiously enough, the identity of one of the persons in the group — an Indian mystic or priest, draped in a piece of white loincloth, with a string of black beads around his neck and a distinctive marking on his forehead, continues to elude me to this day. Ironically, just the fact that I am unable to ascertain his identity has helped strengthen my conviction that what I had 'seen' was in fact *real*, and not a projection of my own mind upon the ethers of the astral world. Logically speaking, had he been a product of my conscious mind, then his identity should have been readily known to me and not be the mystery that it still remains.

Similarly, when it came to identifying the last and final person in my group of luminaries that I refer to as my 'star heads,' I again drew a blank. Although I had no idea as to who this person was, instinct told me that he was somehow affiliated to the Greek philosopher, Socrates. Yet, for some reason, the name *Aristocles* kept springing to my lips every time I visualized the image in my head. I naturally assumed it was a slip of the tongue on my part for what I supposed was really 'Aristotle' — one of the prominent Greek philosophers also from that era.

Upon examining a reasonable facsimile of Aristotle's bust, however, I found that it bore no resemblance to the image that I was carrying around in my head. As I searched around for other images that could well fit the bill — including one of Plato, the Greek philosopher who had been an avid student of Socrates, I was stunned to discover that not only had I nailed that last person, but Plato's real or given name was *Aristocles!* Plato meant 'broad,' a nickname that he had acquired during his schooldays due to his broad shoulders and the wide span of his forehead, and was one that he had come to be universally identified with in later years.

This fascinating piece of trivia on Plato, although not earth-shattering in itself, helped convince me that what I had 'seen' or 'heard' actually seemed to have some basis of truth. Like my dreams, little known facts and pieces of information from my experience were slowly beginning to surface that seemed to defy logic and conventional wisdom. And it was becoming increasingly evident to me that what I had, in fact, encountered was a *direct vision* of a totally different kind of reality — one that would have been quite impossible for me to have imagined.

* * *

Although I had no trouble accepting the blessing of direct vision in my life, I nevertheless did feel a little unworthy of having merited such grace. Generally speaking though, I had no qualms about accepting the authenticity of my next group of luminaries — namely, the Prophets Noah, Moses, Jesus, Muhammad, Krishna, Buddha, and the Virgin Mary, as they have always formed an integral part of my system of beliefs. But it was only in *directly* witnessing their inner radiance that I was able to grasp how each was not only a legitimate path to God but, indeed, formed the *essence* that is God.

Moreover, witnessing the manifestation of Krishna as the genuine reincarnation of that four-armed East Indian deity known as *Vishnu*, now seemed more of a privilege than an aberration. Even catching a glimpse of my own less than illustrious personalities from the past seemed more believable now — as the concept of reincarnation for me has always seemed a perfectly sound and logical basis for addressing the issues of growth and personal accountability.

Reincarnation is a universally accepted doctrine in all Eastern religions, one that exists alongside the belief in the survival of the soul after death. I was surprised to learn that it was also a widely accepted belief in Christianity for more than five centuries, before it was struck out from the Bible by the Ecumenical Council and Catholic Church in A.D. 553.

Surprisingly enough, trying to reconcile the vision of the *ovoid* form of my 'emotional self,' too, did not seem as alien or as far-fetched as it had first appeared. In a theosophical pamphlet published by Bishop C.W. Leadbeater in 1895, he spoke of seeing a distinct *"oval mass of luminous mist"* in his observations of the astral world. Incredibly, it seemed to coincide with my own perceptions of 'the emotional self.' More specifically, he noted: *"To the clairvoyant eye, the physical body of a man appears surrounded by what we call the 'aura' — a luminous colored mist, roughly ovoid in shape, and extending to a distance of some eighteen inches from the body in all directions."*

Also, so far as trying to find some kind of reference to that intensely sublime experience of coming face to face with my higher or 'shining self' was concerned, I found several references to the 'resplendent one' in the Persian *Desatir*. The *Desatir* is a collection of writings of the different Persian Prophets, one of whom was Zoroaster — believed to be the first of the wise men, or *Magi*.

I was surprised to learn that it was also a much sought-after ideal amongst the ancient Greeks since the time of Plato and Socrates. In fact, Plotinus — the philosopher of Roman descent born in Egypt in A.D 205, generally considered to be the founder of Neo-Platonism responsible for reviving Plato's works — was said to have united with his radiant *Augoeides* or 'shining self' several times during his own lifetime.

Neo-Platonism, both a philosophy and spiritual tradition based on Plato's teachings, stems from the logical and more humanistic traditions of classical Greek thought that also has elements of mysticism in it. In fact, Plotinus was the first to convey this synthesis of 'western' Greek thought and 'eastern' mysticism in his *Enneads* — a collection of Plotinus' writings compiled by his student Porphyry in A.D. 270.

In it, Plotinus refers to a highly structured hierarchy of spiritual levels that an individual soul has to go through from the physical plane — *before* he can ascend or rise to mystical union with the One through contemplation, or meditation. He further maintained that the Supreme Transcendent One — or God, is not only without division or distinction but *exists beyond all else*, and is that which has to be *experienced* as opposed to being rationally understood.

Neo-Platonism was also an early influence on Christian thinkers like St. Augustine and St. Francis, and remained a strong influence in Europe during the Middle Ages from the 5th to the 15th centuries. It even influenced Jewish thinkers like Maimondes and the Kabbalist Isaac the Blind, as well as Islamic philosophers such as al-Farabi and Avicenna (*Abu ali Sina*). Then with the retrieval and translation of Greek and Arabic texts, it brought increased awareness of Plato's works.

As a result, Neo-Platonism again experienced a resurgence during the time of the Renaissance in several of the Gnostic and esoteric traditions around the world.

What caught me by surprise, however, was the fact that Neo-Platonism was both accepted as well as adopted by the Fatimid dynasty in Egypt during the 11th century, in the time of Fatimid Caliph and Imam *al-Hakim bi Amr Allah* — also the hereditary Imam of the Shia Ismaili Muslims at the time! I further learned that the doctrine of Neo-Platonism was not only taught but also actively promulgated by the Ismaili *da'is*, or missionaries, who formed a vital part of my own spiritual traditions and history. This, in turn, influenced the writings of Ismaili scholar, poet and missionary — Nasir Khusraw, born in Tajikistan (1004-1088 A.D.) and one responsible for spreading *Ismailism* into Central Asia, China, Russia, Afghanistan, Tajikistan, Badakshan, and the Pamirs.

He is to this day venerated as a saint in Central Asia and considered to be one of the great philosophers and poets in Persian literature. The following verse by Nasir Khusraw helps capture the esoteric essence and underlying philosophy of Shia Ismaili thought:

"With an inner vision look at the World's mystery
Our outward sight cannot discover it
This [outer] world is but a staircase to that higher World
Whose steps we have to mount ..."

The deeply mystical overtones in Khusraw's poetry, and the fact that I, too, had encountered very distinct 'steps' or levels in heaven as professed by Plato, Plotinus and Khusraw, and even 'seen' a vision of the Greek philosopher Plato, prompted me to take a closer look at Plato's works and Neo-Platonism itself. I soon realized that there was definitely an aspect to my faith that had its roots in classical *Greek* philosophy — something I had overlooked until now, which could have a profound effect on how I viewed my spiritual beliefs.

Indeed, I was surprised to learn that the cardinal principle at the core of Neo-Platonic philosophy has always included a belief in the One Supreme transcendent God that has existed prior to all existence. Furthermore, according to the Neo-Platonists, God or the One, is both above reason and being and is found *within*, and that *all* souls come from the same Source, God, to whom we shall one day all return.

I further discovered that the concepts of 'unity consciousness' and 'duality' have always been central to Neo-Platonic thought. Moreover, it also places a clear distinction between our lower emotions or 'irrational self' (*nafs*), and the 'higher self' — which forms an integral part of our intellect (*aql*).

But, more than anything else, what caught me totally off-guard was the fact that the Neo-Platonists not only believed in the pre-existence and immortality of the soul, but they also believed in *reincarnation* — something that I had thought was strictly an *Eastern* concept that had originated from my East Indian heritage and beliefs!

Incredibly, it struck me that ALL of these Neo-Platonist beliefs not only resonated with me personally, but seemed to form the basis of my own faith. In fact, I realized that these same attitudes and beliefs were not only fundamental to the tenets of *Shia Ismaili* faith, but Islam itself — depending, of course, on what interpretation of the *Qur'an*, whether *Shia* or *Sunni*, was used.

* * *

It struck me with a sense of profound wonder that my experience had not only bordered on the mystical, but had also drawn upon ancient Greek philosophy. And in order for me to grasp the full essence of what I had experienced, I knew that I would not only have to research the obvious, but that which was less obvious and even deeply mystical.

As I started to study esoteric texts and near-death accounts of individuals from different religious backgrounds, I began to gain a clearer insight into other people's experiences in the Light. What surprised me was the fact that the soul's crowning experience, namely, becoming one with God, was not the exclusive domain of mystics or saints. Ordinary folk from all walks of life — whether in Islam, Christianity, Hinduism, or the Kabbalist sect in Judaism, too, spoke of having a mystical encounter with the Light. But whether they referred to it as *Enlightenment, At-onement, SaachKhand, Sahaj Avasthaa, Santh, Samadi, Anasrava, Fanafillah* — or what is generally known as *Oneness*, was irrelevant. What mattered was the fact that they were all referring to the *same* experience, namely, becoming one with God's Light.

Consequently, I have to admit that my own encounter with the Light was not only subliminally real, but also mathematically probable, due to the greater weight of numbers on my side. All religious and transcendental experiences seemed to point the same way. So even if I were inclined to dismiss or turn a blind eye to some of the less documented aspects of my experience, I knew there was no way that I could ignore the overwhelming abundance of evidence already existing with regard to the experience of *Oneness* itself.

What finally convinced me of my truth, was something that had existed under my nose all along. In studying the translated texts of devotional hymns, or *ginans*, composed by the various Ismaili Pirs who had first introduced Islam to the Indian subcontinent many centuries ago, I made a startling discovery. I uncovered several references to some of my less mainstream experiences right inside the esoteric hearts of these *ginans*. Ironically, they were the same *ginans* that I had recited — both as a child and as an adult, but never really taken the time or trouble to fully understand.

The term *ginan* is derived from the Sanskrit word *jnan*, which means spiritual knowledge, wisdom or gnosis. The Persian term *Pir* means a Sufi master, or spiritual guide who is qualified to lead disciples along the mystical path. The great Ismaili Pirs — like Pir Satgur Noor, Pir Sadardin, Pir Shams and Pir Hassan Kabirdin, who had travelled to India since the 11th century, had imparted such spiritual knowledge to their converts by composing hymns or *ginans* in their native language, in a manner that they could easily understand. It was not until the latter part of the 20th century, however, that several of these *ginans* were rendered into English from their local dialects and circulated amongst the fifteen million members of the Ismaili community worldwide.

Laying my hands on the translated texts of these precious *ginans* was like striking spiritual gold. As I started to slowly digest and assimilate the information contained in these *ginans,* all the missing pieces of the celestial puzzle in my head finally started to fall into place. More importantly, it was a relief just to know that I was not coming out from left field like I had initially supposed! I now had in my hands 'proof positive' that I was no longer alone in my experience. There were individuals, venerated in their own right, who claimed to have experienced what I had experienced. Fortunately for me, they had rendered it for all posterity in a beautifully moving and poetic form that had managed to stand the test of time.

* * *

One of the first pieces of gnostic wisdom to catch my eye was reference to a spiritual bath or 'light shower' in a *ginan* (*Sakhee Mahaapad Keree Vaat*) composed by Pir Sadardin. In it, he spoke of experiencing a mystical and exalted state when the two subtle energy systems in our body (*Ingla* and *Pingla*) were united with the central (*Sukhmana*) nerve in meditation. He described the spontaneous union of these two energy systems in our body in terms of *'a sprinkling of glitter and light'* that brought forth a 'spiritual awakening' in the individual.

The dazzling shower of light according to the Pir heralded a 'rebirth' or the inauguration of a soul from a lower life into a higher life. In essence, it represented a 'spiritual baptism' where the individual soul was cleansed of all its impurities under the 'shower of light' — *before* being allowed to proceed further into the higher realms of reality.

In reading the translated text of this particular *ginan*, I was reminded of my own experience under the 'shower of light,' just prior to discovering the radiance of my own soul. Upon further research I came across a *ginan* composed by Pir Shams (*Raja Goverchand Akhyan*), in which he categorically stated that once you had killed your ego — or *'emotional self,'* you would be amazed to learn that you, yourself, were a part and parcel of God's Light!

Solid references to the ego and our potential to become a part of God's Light, along with references to a 'glitter shower' in these *ginans* definitely aroused my interest. It compelled me to dig deeper and research further into these intriguing aspects of my experience. I soon discovered that there is a 'light force' — known as the *kundalini,* which normally lies dormant in us. And the activation of this sacred 'light force' has, since time immemorial, been universally acknowledged as being the point of true 'awakening' in an individual.

What intrigued me was the fact that this process of self-realization, or the awakening of this subtle energy within us, has been the goal of *all* esoteric traditions around the world. Adherents of the *Hatha* or *Sahaja Yoga,* a form of meditative yoga, too, make reference to the union of the *Ingla* and the *Pingla* to help unleash this sacred light force in us known as the *kundalini,* to attain spiritual salvation. This same goal is also said to be achieved by channeling the subtle male and female energies in us — as represented by the Sun and the Moon respectively — through the seven *chakras* or energy centers around our body.

Similarly, I discovered that the Chinese form of meditation known as *Tai Chi* also aims at balancing one's *yin* and *yang* — which again represent the male and female energies in our bodies, to help activate this *same* life force in us known as *chi*. Bringing the two energies into balance is said to promote physical and mental well-being as well as a greater spiritual awareness within ourselves.

Apart from its prevalence in Eastern traditions, I was amazed to learn that the Mayan God, *Quetzalcoatl,* too, was portrayed with a plumage around his head representing the sacred rays of this *same* life force emanating from his crown. This 'life force' is also seen in Western cultures in the form of the *'caduceus'* — a common symbol in medicine today derived from Greek mythology. According to legend, Hermes the winged messenger of the Greek God Zeus, always carried with him a golden *caduceus,* or magic staff, surmounted by wings and two snakes. This symbol of intertwined snakes represents the two subtle energies in our bodies, something that also appeared in early Babylonia where it was commonly regarded as a symbol of wisdom and healing among its gods.

* * *

In thinking back to my own experience, it occurred to me that this shimmering 'life force' in me had somehow been spontaneously activated during the time of my 'death' in Florida. Among other things, it had manifested itself as a sudden explosion of love, light and healing within me, along with a deeper understanding of life itself.

Oddly enough, even in the midst of this magnificent spectacle of light, I remember yearning for something more. Although the razzle-dazzle and razzmatazz of the higher dimensions had certainly been fascinating and captivating to my senses, something inside had intuitively informed me that this was *not* the ultimate or crowning experience. Even seeing a fleeting image of myself as a 'spiritual bride' joyously awaiting the call to the side of her Beloved, amidst great fanfare, had seemed somewhat fanciful to me.

Seeing a vivid vision of myself being ushered into the Light as a 'glowing bride' was, therefore, not something I felt I could take too seriously as it did not seem material in terms of my overall experience in the spirit world. But I was, nevertheless, vaguely aware that this type of intensely personal relationship between a Master and his disciple — often portrayed as a lover interacting with her Beloved, was a perfectly valid and well-trodden path to God in Sufism and other mystical branches in Islam.

Upon further research, I discovered that for the Sufis and esoteric sects in Islam like my own, as well as other mystical traditions in Christianity and Judaism, God is not only the *Oneness* of all that is — namely, both the Manifest and the Mystery, but also *LOVE* that resonates inside the human heart. In fact, according to these traditions a kind of 'mystical union' or 'mystical marriage' can occur purely as a result of the love and longing in one's heart for God, or the Beloved.

It was not until I seriously started to study other translated texts of *ginans* from my own tradition such as those composed by the Ismaili Pir Sadardin, however, that I came across pointed references to a mystical 'bridal' experience that caught me totally by surprise. In them, the Pir describes the momentous experience of *Oneness* in terms of seeing oneself as a 'spiritual bride' *(visav kunvari)*, being wedded to the Lord *(Shahna lagan)* on an occasion of great festivity and light *(mandavo)*. Moreover, he emphasized that the vision would be so bright and so vivid, that it would have the power to eliminate all doubt in one's mind about the true veracity of that experience.

Uncovering this rare piece of spiritual lore completely blew me away. Indeed, it served to remove all traces of doubt in my mind as to the authenticity of my experience. I knew then with absolute conviction in my heart, that what I had experienced was, in fact, *real* and the closest I had come to experiencing the Truth. I realized that I no longer needed *intellectual* 'proof' for what I knew to be empirically true — namely, something that has to be *experienced* in order for it to be fully understood.

* * *

In finally embracing my truth, I knew that I had experienced reality at its best. Like Shakespeare before me, I made the supreme realization that there are, indeed, *more things in heaven and earth than are dreamt of in our philosophy.* There are definite aspects to life, as well as death, that not only defy our present system of logic and understanding, but are incapable of being perceived through our *physical* senses.

It dawned on me that I was really a transcendentalist at heart, like many others before me — including people such as Emanuel Swedenborg, the German Romantics, English poets and writers like Shakespeare, Wordsworth, Coleridge, Carlyle, Blake and Yeats, as well as thinkers like Goethe, Immanuel Kant, Hegel, Carl Jung, Henry David Thoreau, and Ralph Waldo Emerson — father of the transcendental movement in America.

According to the transcendentalists, knowledge is not only derived from our physical senses, but also through intuition, personal reflection and contemplation. Charles Mayo Ellis captures the essence of what it is to be a 'transcendentalist' in a pamphlet that he published in 1842 entitled 'An Essay on Transcendentalism,' in which he categorically states: *"Transcendentalism maintains that man has ideas that come not through the five senses or the power of reasoning, but are either the result of direct revelation from God, his immediate inspiration, or his immanent presence in the spiritual world, and it asserts that man has something besides the body of flesh — a spiritual body, with senses to perceive what is true, right and beautiful ..."*

I realized, however, that my quest for knowledge via the 'power of reasoning' had not been entirely in vain. It was only through the vehicle of my *intellectual* search that I was able to appreciate the power of conviction and personal experience over pure reasoning in my life. Not only had it helped me acknowledge the mystical — or that which is hidden, but it helped me make that great leap of faith from the shadows of my intellectual rhetoric into the light-filled domain of true intuitive knowledge and wisdom.

Ironically, had it not been for the anomalies in my experience and the intellectual curiosity that they aroused in me, I would not have embarked upon my present course of inquiry. This rhetorical inquiry — or *Socratic Method* of self-questioning to arrive at the truth, helped to definitively convince me of my own truth and vision of the afterlife. In a strange sort of way, the very anomalies that had confounded me had served to ultimately point me towards the Truth.

* * *

The fact that I had experienced 'death' — or that point of highest consciousness in an individual, at the Celebration Health Hospital in Orlando, was not a coincidence. It was just a positive testament and affirmation of the hospital's central philosophy on the role of the Divine in our lives.

In conducting my own research into the state-of-the-art facility known as Celebration Health, opened in 1998 — the same year that I was admitted there, I discovered that it was founded on strong Adventist principles of health that actively honored our connection to a loving God. Above all, it professed an absolute faith and trust in the power of Divine intervention in the healing process. I believe I am living proof of that intervention.

This synthesis, or coming together of faith and science where faith in God co-exists alongside medical science, is the prime focus of health and healing at Celebration Health. It is not a question of either/or but *both* having a valid place in the tending of human life. I am convinced that this unique blending of scientific expertise with an open declaration of faith in God at Celebration Health, helped create the ideal conditions in my case for the will of the Divine to be worked through the miracle of modern science.

I now know that there is no such thing as a 'coincidence' or chance happening in life. Everything in life happens for a reason and by design. Even my encounter with death was not an 'accident' or some cosmic mistake just waiting to happen, but a blessing in disguise that helped open my eyes to an *inner* world of truth and beauty that I barely knew existed. It was God's mysterious way of waking me up to the truth and our true state of being — which is spirit, or *light*.

Discovering this truth in the unlikeliest of places — *within myself* — made me realize that I did not necessarily have to travel halfway around the world to be awakened to a new kind of awareness, or discover that great and amazing truth that the kingdom of God lies within.

William Blake — the 18th century poet, painter, mystic and Neo-Platonist following in the tradition of Plato, Jesus, St. Francis and Rumi, among others — always tried to open our eyes to a Higher Reality and the *inner* world of spirit in his creative works. His words seem to ring eternally true:

> *"For all Men are in Eternity ...*
> *In your own Bosom you bear*
> *your Heaven and Earth & all you behold;*
> *tho' it appears Without, it is Within,*
> *in your Imagination*
> *of which this World of Mortality*
> *is but a Shadow."*

This type of mystical consciousness — often referred to as excluded knowledge or 'Perennial Philosophy,' invites us to awaken to a Higher spiritual reality. Moreover, not only have mystics been found throughout the ages, but this type of philosophy has always been present, in one form or another, in all the great schools of mysticism around the world. It has been known by several names — Hermeticism, Philosophia, Neo-Platonism, Illuminism, Kabbala, Sufism, Gnosticism and Esotericism.

In fact, in looking back, I realized that my own faith *Shia Ismaili Islam* has, in all its fourteen hundred years of history, always been an 'esoteric' faith. A closer look at some of the mystical traditions around the world that have also looked to the 'essence' or *spirit*, as opposed to strict religious dogma, not only revealed some basic universal truths, but brought to light the one underlying principle that unites us all — a common yearning to *experience* the Divine.

* * *

Ironically, in an age of great scientific and technological advancement, as well as material plenty, we are still left searching for the meaning of life. Such perennial wisdom from the ages can, no doubt, help shine a convincing and much needed light on that which we call 'reality' — where *spirit*, and the inner world of our thought and imagination, can once again become a part of our dominant reality.

I now know that there is an infinitely higher purpose running through our seemingly mundane and existential lives on earth. Our main challenge, it seems, lies in trying to contemplate the mundane in order to understand the Divine. Thus, cultivating a healthy understanding of the nature and purpose of this duality, as well as that intrinsic duality of mind and matter in our lives, can go a long way towards helping us reconcile our outer world to our inner world. While one is visible, the other is not — yet it holds the key to the truth about life itself.

Having experienced a state of consciousness that goes *beyond* duality and transcends thought itself, has given me a greater appreciation for life here on Earth as well as the higher spiritual life that awaits us all. If, for the sake of argument, my 'experience' was a dream and a figment of my imagination, then it is the clearest, most profoundly life-changing dream that I could ever have hoped for. It has illuminated my life in ways that I would never have dreamt was possible. Above all, it has been my direct path to the understanding of the Truth.

Awakening in death has helped me awaken more fully to life as, paradoxically, death explains life. Only in coming face to face with my own death have I realized what *life* is about. Ultimately, unveiling the mystery of death and the role of the Divine in our lives holds the answers to life itself — which is but a short passage in eternity. Yet, it is a journey that we all have to necessarily undertake, and endure, for the sake of our *spirit* and the very essence of who we are.

About the Author

Azmina Suleman was born in Nairobi, Kenya, and moved to England during her late teens before immigrating to Canada in 1981. She worked in the legal field in Calgary, Alberta, for several years before graduating in journalism and taking up writing professionally. She has a Master's degree in legal history and is also the author of the book *"In the Name of Justice — Portrait of a Cowboy Judge,"* a biography of the former Chief Justice of the Trial Division of Alberta, James Valentine Hogarth Milvain, O.C., Q.C., LL.D.

As a Shia Ismaili Muslim and follower of His Highness Prince Karim Aga Khan IV — spiritual leader and hereditary Imam of fifteen million Ismaili Muslims around the world, she felt compelled to take a closer look at some of the more mystical and esoteric aspects of her near-death experience. This led her into an entirely new branch of research and an in-depth look at the phenomenon of near-death experiences, as well as the field of consciousness studies generally. This book is the direct result of that search and her personal quest for the truth. She has two sons and lives with her husband in Calgary, Alberta.

Testimonials

Azmina Suleman weaves together a personal account of her near-death experience with the wisdom of scripture. Even though we are of the Roman Catholic faith, Azmina's book speaks to all faiths alike as she makes us realize that we are all equally children of the ONE God, and that we are all in it together on our journey through life. My husband George, 68 years, who has never read a book from cover to cover in his life, is now reading *A Passage to Eternity* for the second time! *B.D. Calgary, Alberta*

Ms. Suleman's book, *A Passage to Eternity*, has changed my life. I feel a greater sense of connection with all people as I realize that we are ALL, indeed, one with God. *G.C. Morley, Alberta*

A Passage to Eternity captivated me right from the start with its philosophical insights and clear moments of epiphany. It is an inspiring account of a profound mystical experience, yet it is written in a language that is easy to follow and understand. Reading Azmina's book has opened my heart and mind to a whole new dimension of wisdom and thought. It is one book that has managed to touch me deeply, and one that I can say is truly out of this world. *S.F. Calgary, Alberta*

One of the first things that struck me about Azmina's book, *A Passage to Eternity*, was its disarming honesty and candor. It is a very well-written book; its lucid style of prose and fluency makes it both readable and at the same time engaging, and one that compels you to read at one sitting. In a word, this book is nothing short of phenomenal. *J.P. Calgary, Alberta*

Azmina has managed to convey her highly emotional experience in a logical and thought-provoking manner. A book that is hard to put down. It is a very uplifting book that is sure to be of great interest and comfort to many, as it offers you an entirely new perspective on life. *R.K. Calgary, Alberta*

A Passage to Eternity is truly a gift to the world. It is a book that mystifies and amazes, and challenges you to think "outside the box." It sheds light on our true purpose in life and conveys a message of hope and harmony amongst all people on Earth. The language is both powerful and inspiring, as well as intellectually and emotionally uplifting. It is a book that shares immense knowledge, yet, leaves you asking for more. In a nutshell, it is a book that touches your soul. *R.M. Calgary, Alberta*

Azmina Suleman's book allows us to journey deep into the realms of our own spirituality, as it provides reassurances of an absolute Divine intervention after death. Aboriginal spiritual revelations parallel those experienced by Azmina. The powerful belief of a continuance of spirit after death and the ascension into a greater spiritual realm of being have long been a strong element of native culture. Azmina's amazing story inspires and compels us to truly contemplate our own journey through life. *D.M. Morley, Alberta*

Thank you so much for introducing me to Azmina Suleman's wonderful book, *A Passage to Eternity*. The book is a real eye-opener on spirituality. I gave the book to a colleague at work and she was so intrigued by it that she bought her own! *N.C. Ottawa, Ontario*

A Passage to Eternity is one of the best books I have read. It has changed my whole outlook on life and the way I understand life. I recently lent my copy to a friend who was going abroad, but as I read parts of it on a regular basis, I realized I was left without a book! Thank you for writing such an inspirational book. You have brought hope and encouragement to many. *S.S. Nairobi, Kenya*

A Passage to Eternity is a real page-turner. From the moment I laid my eyes on the book cover, I was drawn. It made me laugh. It made me cry. It made me think. It made me reflect. It cast a renewed light on my beliefs. I could almost hear her voice as I read, which completely blew me away. Her vivid descriptions had the power to simply transport me to another realm.

F.K. St. John's, Newfoundland

I have read many, many books on spiritual enlightenment, on how and what path one should take in life in order to experience the glory of God. But none of them have touched me as powerfully or as deeply as Azmina's extraordinary book, *A Passage to Eternity*. There is a kind of mystical beauty and power in her written word. My mind is still reeling with the eloquence of the words with which she describes her experience. One of my perennial questions has always been about our purpose in life and what our mission in life entails. She is the first person who has addressed what the phrase 'purpose in life' or one's 'mission in life' truly means. I believe her book is going to have a huge impact on our times. Its powerful message prods us to awaken to our own potential for attaining true enlightenment.   *N.J. Calgary, Alberta*

A Passage to Eternity grips you from the start, making you want to keep on reading it to the end. The flow and articulation in the book makes you feel like you are taking the journey with her yourself, and helps you dispel your fear of death as you see what's on the other side. Her book has made me realize that life is a blessing and something that should never be taken for granted.
                    A.S. Calgary, Alberta

From the moment I started to read Azmina's book, I could not put it down. It felt like as if she were by my side reading every word to me. One of the things that really spoke to me was what she reveals about prayer benefitting both the person being prayed for, as well as the person praying. I was surprised to learn that it also benefits me! It is like getting a gift back from God when I did not expect it. Wow! We often get so caught up in ourselves trying to heal our own pain that we cannot see that the simple answer we are looking for is right in front of us — service. Azmina's book has absolutely convinced me that service is "love in action" which will not only heal us, but ultimately heal the world. Thank you for writing this beautiful book. I will treasure it always.
                    A.F. Calgary, Alberta

It is an excellent first-hand account of an afterlife experience. The book grips you from the beginning and by the time you reach the end you are convinced.   *F.I. Toronto, Ontario*

I am of no specific religion but have been searching for the truth since I was a young girl. I have read hundreds of books on philosophy, spirituality and near-death experiences. My son who was 23 years old was tragically killed in a car accident several weeks ago. With all of the wisdom and spirituality that I have gained through life, I still find it difficult to go on in this world without him. I am very grateful to have found *A Passage to Eternity* for the message of hope and great solace that it brings. I cannot thank Azmina enough for sharing her experiences. *D.H. Belleville, Ontario*

A Passage to Eternity is a real eye opener. It demystified death for me and helped me understand the stages that a soul goes through before it reaches its final destination. It was especially relevant for me as I just lost my dear father three months ago. The book has helped many other people that I know of who have also lost their loved ones. They, too, found answers that they were looking for in the book. I have no words to express my gratitude. Thank you for writing such a wonderful book and helping us understand the other world better. *N.M. Montreal, Quebec*

A Passage to Eternity is a wonderful book that offers a vivid and detailed account of the journey of our souls. It explains the way in which our souls communicate in the hereafter, and assures us that our loved ones and those dearest to us provide us with loving support in the life hereafter. I have always wondered what happened to us when we passed on and I have definitely found the answer in Azmina's book! Thank you so much for sharing your extraordinary experience with us. *N.D. Mississauga, Ontario*

Azmina Suleman shines a convincing light on a complex multi-dimensional world and the journey of the soul into the life hereafter. But in spite of the complexity of the subject matter, she has managed to convey it simply and in a language that is both easy to read and understand. Even our teenage daughter in high school was clearly able to grasp the message in her book. We have learned a lot from Azmina's journey and can now relate better to some of the events in our own lives.

Z.H. & H.H. Calgary, Alberta

Azmina Suleman has truly succeeded in putting into words a profound spiritual experience. An awe-inspiring account of personal enlightenment, *A Passage to Eternity* offers a rare glimpse of a cosmic reality to all soul-searching seekers of the truth.

S.T. Ruston, Louisiana

A Passage to Eternity has helped me accept the challenges in my life gracefully. I am now grateful for those lessons as I embrace change and challenge in my life. I realize that life is truly a gift. The message in Azmina's book has been incredibly freeing for me. It has helped remove the need for judgment of my own past and that of others as well. I cannot thank her enough for communicating this in her book.

V.K. Calgary, Alberta

I have read many New Age and spiritual books, but Azmina's book *A Passage to Eternity* goes further. It describes her actual experience in a manner that is easy to read and follow. I have often wondered why most near-death accounts have primarily been written by Christians, and why people from other faiths have not been more forthcoming with such knowledge. Thank you, Azmina, for having the courage to share your personal experiences with us.

P.M. Calgary, Alberta

I have read many, many books on near-death experiences. But all of them have been a collection of glimpses by the author of *other* near-death experiencers. What attracted me to this book was that it was the first book that I came across that had such a detailed description of an NDE — one that the author had *personally* experienced and written herself. The strength of this book is the honesty with which the author has dealt with the subject.

S.N. Lenexa, Kansas

An account of a near-death experience like you've never had explained to you before! Azmina captures the most intimate details of an extraordinary event in her life and conveys it in such a way that you feel you have been granted a passage on an intimate voyage of discovery yourself. Emotionally captivating, a mystery slowly unveiled, it is an inspiring, moment-by-moment account of one woman's awakening.

C.M. Calgary, Alberta

A Passage to Eternity transports the reader into the transcendental realms of the 'Real World,' as it endorses the esoteric interpretation of scriptures of all faiths. It informs us that it is a world to which ALL souls will one day return. If by chance this book comes across as a work of fiction, then it is one of the most well-articulated and brilliantly crafted pieces of fiction that I have ever come across. The stunning clarity, the flow of thought and the language used, however, belies it to be a work of fiction as it shimmers with esoteric wisdom — something that can only come from a world beyond.   *K.J. Mississauga, Ontario*

A Passage to Eternity gives us a real glimpse into the world of spirituality, as it describes the intricate process that a soul passes through as it marks its trajectory towards its ultimate merging with the Almighty. The most redeeming feature of the book is its confirmation that ALL religions steeped in the practice of the universal principles of charity, kindness, patience and self-betterment lead the soul towards its inevitable destiny — the journey back Home. Translating the intricacies of the world of spirit into an earthly language is as challenging as having a mute describe the hue of a color to a blind man. Yet, Azmina comes close to accomplishing this. This book promises to inspire and spark a light within all those who read the book.   *S.L. Calgary, Alberta*

AN EXCELLENT READ!! Azmina Suleman writes so beautifully that you feel you are there with her sharing her experience. A very vivid account of a Near-Death Experience that brings the reader closer to understanding our purpose in life. Azmina explains how all paths are the way to the ONE true God and how all humanity has been guided and loved from the onset of its birth experience. Stimulating reading for the hearts and minds of those who open the pages of this book looking for enlightenment.

Angels1111 Westcoast, USA

CPSIA information can be obtained
at www.ICGtesting.com
Printed in the USA
BVHW042032100220
571961BV00009BA/196